SIMON COWELL

THE MAN WHO CHANGED THE WORLD

SIMON COWELL

THE MAN WHO CHANGED THE WORLD

DAVID NOLAN

JOHN BLAKE

Published by John Blake Publishing Ltd,
3 Bramber Court, 2 Bramber Road,
London W14 9PB, England

www.johnblakepublishing.co.uk

First published in paperback in 2010

ISBN: 978 1 84454 987 0

British Library Cataloguing-in-Publication Data:

A catalogue record for this book is available from the British Library.

Design by www.envydesign.co.uk

Printed in Great Britain by Bookmarque Ltd, Croydon. CR0 4TD

1 3 5 7 9 10 8 6 4 2

Papers used by John Blake Publishing are natural, recyclable products made
from wood grown in sustainable forests. The manufacturing processes
conform to the environmental regulations of the country of origin.

ABOUT THE AUTHOR

David Nolan is a former journalist and producer with ITV and the author of *You're Entitled to an Opinion – The High Times and Many Lives of Tony Wilson, Factory Records and the Haçienda.* He has also written biographies on Blur singer Damon Albarn and New Order front man Bernard Sumner. His first book, *I Swear I Was There: The Gig That Changed The World*, was named as one of the top 50 music books of all time by *GQ* magazine.

Thanks to Elstree studio historian Paul Welsh, as well as Pat Strack from Elstree and Borehamwood Council for their help, and thanks especially to Pauline Hosiers for her help with the Great Abbots Mead Mystery. I'm also grateful to Lucian Randall for pointing me in the direction of this book and to editor Amy McCulloch at John Blake Publishing.

For Katherine – here's one The Queen might actually get to know about.

CONTENTS

INTRO
EAST LONDON –
20 JANUARY 2010

We are backstage at the National Television Awards at the O2 Arena in London's Docklands. Britain's TV industry is doing what it does best – glad handing, air kissing and congratulating itself. Business as usual.

In the dressing rooms and communal areas, TV monitors show a feed of what's happening on stage. In front of an enormous, hyped-up crowd the usual suspects are getting their gongs: Ant and Dec, outgoing Doctor Who David Tennant and *Gavin and Stacey* writer and star James Corden.

But some of the screens aren't tuned to the prizegiving: they're switched to 24-hour news channels. What's more, they show very different pictures – rolling news images of the horror caused by a devastating earthquake in Haiti eight days earlier, flickering silently as the party gets started for the television stars and their producers.

One man, clutching an award for Most Popular Talent Show, watches the pain on the faces of the Haitian survivors. Even the hardest of hearts can't fail to be touched by the human disaster that's on display – and this man's heart is famously harder than just about anyone's.

A plan has started to form in his mind and a high-profile event such as this is the perfect opportunity for him to start putting it into action. He holds court, something he is clearly very used to. 'I'm literally making this up as we go along,' he tells reporters in a corridor outside the room set aside for press interviews. 'We've put the word out, we'll see what comes in over the next two or three days. I don't know who's available but I will get a record out in the next seven to ten days. The Prime Minister called me a couple of days ago and said if we put a record out he'll waive the VAT. It's not the best time because logistically we're all over the place.'

As the head of a billion-pound music and TV business, this man has a schedule that's a globally punishing one. As well as picking up television awards in London, he's fulfilling filming commitments for *Britain's Got Talent* around the UK, and the ninth season of *American Idol* – the last he is to be involved with – has just gone on air in the US. Then there's the small matter of his music company Syco, with artists such as Susan Boyle, Leona Lewis, Il Divo and Westlife to look after. 'How difficult is this going to be for you?' asks one journalist. 'Not as difficult as the time *they're* having,' he replies, without missing a beat. 'I will make it happen.'

No one doubts the man for a second. After all, he's Simon Cowell. He's changed the world. And he's about to do it again.

ONE

*I CAN'T REFUSE
THE TASK*

Tiptoeing through the shrubs and bushes, the little boy
felt drawn to the buzz of light and noise that seemed
to glow from his neighbour's house. The young Simon
Cowell loved nothing better than to peer over the garden
fence of his childhood home in the village of Elstree, north
of London. It would take him a little longer than most kids
to get to the garden fence, as the detached property he and
his family lived in was set on five acres of land. But it was
worth the trek, because of what he saw on the other side.

By any standards to be expected in the early 1960s, the
Cowells were comfortably off. Their home Abbots Mead
was an eight-bedroomed affair with a separate lodge
house. It was tended by a gardener and a cleaner, and the
family had a live-in nanny. They took several holidays
abroad each year – one would be in Bermuda – so they
knew luxury when they saw it. But the view little Simon got
of his neighbours' homes from over that fence was
something altogether different. It was like spying on
another, even more glamorous, planet.

On one side of the Cowell sprawl their neighbour was Gerry Blatner, the UK boss of Warner Brothers. If a star was in town, plying their trade at the nearby film studios at Elstree and Borehamwood, they were sure to find themselves being entertained in some style at Blatner's house. In later years Simon Cowell would recall stars such as Richard Burton, Gregory Peck, Robert Mitchum and, particularly, Roger Moore – who was filming the hit sixties TV show *The Saint* – descending on the upmarket village.

But there was more. On the other side of Abbots Mead was British movie star Joan Collins and her then husband, the singer and actor Anthony Newley. The pair had settled into the adjoining property, Friars Mead, in 1964 after Joan gave birth to her first child. The noise, laughter and glamour that wafted over the Cowell fence from both sides during those evening spying missions would have a profound effect on the boy. 'As a kid, I would look over the fence at this great house and see everyone – Robert Mitchum, Elizabeth Taylor, all these great actors – having the time of their lives,' Cowell later recalled in an interview with journalist Stephen Armstrong. 'I remember thinking from a very, very early age, "God, I hope I grow up and have a nice house so I can have parties like that."'

It was at those moments, peering at these creatures from another planet, that Simon Cowell decided that he wanted to get into show business.

The extended, slightly convoluted family that Simon Cowell was born into already had a fair few touches of showbiz of its own. His mother – known to all as Julie –

was born Josie Dalglish in 1925 and had been an actress and dancer from an early age, performing under the name Julie Brett. Her first marriage was to a fellow performer – an actor named Bertram. The marriage wasn't to last long but did produce two children, Michael and Tony. The boys were very young when the split came.

Simon's father, Eric Cowell, was some seven years older than Julie. He was a raffish estate agent who also already had two children – John and June. Eric's marriage faltered when the children were aged five and four. June was a stage school girl, a contemporary of Francesca Annis, Susan George and Judy Geeson. She recalls being taken to film sets in a Bentley as a child. She appeared in the 1957 prisoner-of-war drama *Seven Thunders,* but her most memorable performance was in the cult science-fiction chiller *Village of the Damned*, playing one of a group of blonde-haired alien children taking over a sleepy English village. The film was released in 1960 to great critical acclaim and commercial success, but June was to lose her taste for performing in her teens, finding the attention she received from men in the industry distasteful.

Mum Julie was outgoing, the life and soul of the party. According to Simon, interviewed in *The Times* in 2007, she was, 'A creature of the 1960s. She absolutely typified that whole Jackie Onassis glamorous look. Very energetic, very vivacious, very camp. During that time, she was in her element.'

Julie would love to tell the story of her silent, elongated courtship with Eric. Each week, Julie would travel by train to visit her mother. Always accompanied by a female friend, she would often notice a dark-haired, well-dressed man who took the same train. This continued for a full two years until, on one occasion, Julie's friend couldn't make it, and she made the trip alone. Eric saw his chance and took it, asking the young mum out for a drink. They became a couple soon afterwards but didn't marry until 1961.

Eric and Julie already had three boys and a girl between them, but wanted children together to complete their family. It would prove to be a long, difficult process. Although she became pregnant quickly, complications arose and at eight months she had a baby boy by Caesarean section. The poorly child, named Stephen, would, sadly, survive for only one week. Julie and Eric continued with their attempts to add to their family and, after two more miscarriages and ongoing hormone treatment, Julie became pregnant once more – again there were complications and she was hospitalised, convinced that things were set to go badly wrong once again.

When Simon was born on 7 October 1959, Julie still feared her baby wouldn't survive. When it became clear the youngster would pull through, Eric Cowell insisted that his wife put aside her dreams of a show-business career and concentrate on being a full-time mum. 'He wanted me to stop and, by then, I wanted to as well,' Julie later told journalist Jenny Johnston. 'I had a happy home life for the first time, and I wanted to be a full-time mother. It was just a wonderful, happy environment.'

The British musical landscape that existed when Simon Cowell was born was very different from the one he would seismically shift in years to come. Shirley Bassey, Adam Faith and new kid on the block Cliff Richard were the order of the day. The Number 1 song on everyone's lips in October 1959 was Bobby Darin's 'Mack the Knife' – the very song that Simon would later name as his favourite of all time on Radio 4's *Desert Island Discs* programme.

Elvis Presley had exploded onto the worldwide stage three years earlier, but was by now cooling his heels in the US Army. Cowell would later recall being impressed how Presley – and particularly his manager Colonel Tom Parker – harnessed the power of television to boost record sales.

This was a pre-Beatles world waiting for the 1960s to happen – indeed John Lennon, Paul McCartney and George Harrison were still playing in a band called Johnny and the Moondogs in 1959. When they became The Beatles, they too would have an enormous hold on Simon Cowell, not just for their songs or clothes but for what they represented: that there was no limit to how famous you could become or how celebrated your work could be. 'The Beatles were the first band to be photographed living it up in what we now perceive as a traditional rock star fashion,' Cowell would later write in his book about show business *I Don't Mean To Be Rude, But* ... 'For the first time young people looked at them and thought wistfully: that could be me.'

Television was still limited at the end of the fifties, with just two channels on offer. One of the most popular shows of the period was the BBC's *Top Town*. It had an interesting format: a panel, made up of a singer (Vera Lynn), a band leader (Eric Robinson) and a showbiz entrepreneur (Leslie MacDonnell), went on the road judging the undiscovered talent on offer in various parts of the country. How quaint – it could never work today ...

Simon had been born in Brighton – Julie Cowell still lives there today – but the family, with its complex series of step-relationships to accommodate, settled in Elstree after Eric came across the dilapidated Abbots Mead mansion house and decided to renovate it. With a high wall and heavy gates at the front of the property and woodland and views across a valley to the rear, this was an impressive Georgian home by anyone's standards.

'My earliest memory of Simon is me pushing him in a big pram along Elstree High Street,' Simon's half brother Tony told the *Daily Mail* in 2007. 'I adored him, but I hated taking him out because of the pram. It was the 1960s and everything was a sort of pink then. I found that, if I pushed him really fast, swerving in and out along the pavement, he laughed. The faster I went, the more he laughed. He was about two. Simon's very into speed and fast cars now, and we reckon that was his introduction to it.'

By then Julie had given birth again – another boy named Nicholas. He was just 18 months younger than Simon, and the boys were so close in age and looks that they were mistaken for twins. They were even dressed alike to complete the illusion. 'We were brought up practically like twins,' Nicholas later told the *Mail on Sunday*. 'Simon is 18 months older than me but I was always bigger for my age, and, once we hit three or four, we were pretty much the same size. We were seriously competitive and both of us were also pretty obsessed with money. From a really young age, we had to work for our pocket money from Mum. We'd do anything – washing cars, carol singing, mowing lawns, whatever. Neither of us was remotely into saving money in those days – that was boring. We'd spend it on cigarettes and sweets. We were always together, always taking the mick out of each other.'

The pair were as thick as thieves, be it by entertaining the rest of the family by putting on plays and shows, or driving them mad with their bad behaviour – and it would always be Simon leading the charge when it came to wrongdoing. 'Simon was completely out of control as a kid – a real prankster' was how half-brother Michael described Simon in an interview with the *Mirror*. 'He first caused problems as a baby and wouldn't sleep. From then on he completely ruled the roost. He had a gilded childhood and was completely fearless. Nothing has really changed in that respect.' Michael himself moved out of the Cowell household by the age of 15.

'I used to babysit Simon and Nicholas when Dad and Julie went out, and it was a nightmare,' Simon's half-sister June later recalled in an interview with journalist Alison Smith-Squire. 'They were terribly naughty. They would pretend they were asleep, then creep out of bed and open the front door, leaving it ajar. I would run around the house frantically searching, thinking they were wandering around outside. Then I'd hear muffled giggling and discover the pair of them would be hiding in a linen basket.'

Nicholas would be press-ganged into whatever crackpot scheme his brother would conjure up. In fact he would be involved in Simon's first venture into music – and his first experience of music criticism. 'He formed a band with his brother and two friends,' mum Julie later revealed to *New!* magazine. 'We were on holiday in the Caribbean once and he convinced the hotel to let them play. They were awful!'

As they got older, Simon's and Nicholas's behaviour would become more and more cavalier. 'There was a disused chicken run [in the grounds] and Nicholas and I took it over as our camp,' Simon later recalled in an interview with the *Sunday Times*. 'We pinched booze from our parents, put optics on the bottles, and hung them from strings. It was our own pub; we'd take in girls, and smoke and drink. But Mum looked inside one day. I came back to find our den demolished and our goodies gone. I was furious.'

You could perhaps forgive Simon for wanting a taste of the high life.

At home Simon would see his Cuban-cigar-chomping dad Eric jump into his E-type Jag every day and zoom into London like a Home Counties Austin Powers, returning home from work in the mid-evening to hear about the day's adventures. In his absence, Julie – with the help of nanny Heather – ruled the household the best she could, but, with up to six kids in and out of the house at any one time, it was a tall order. Older half-brother Tony would be upstairs in his top-floor room, door firmly shut in true sulky-teen mode, the smell of cigarettes and the sound of Bob Dylan and the

Beach Boys wafting temptingly from inside. His other half-brothers, John and Michael, would be doing their own thing. Sister June was a regular visitor from her natural mum's house. All the children were treated equally and fairly – June in particular would regard Julie as her second mum.

Simon would later describe life at the rambling house off Barnet Lane in Elstree as 'privileged and artistically rich' and say that, despite the complex relationships within his extended family, they were a tight-knit bunch: 'Incredibly close, yes, really close,' he told CNN in 2006. 'My brothers, my sister, my mum and dad … I mean we were more like an Italian family I would say.'

At the head of this 'Italian' family were of course Eric and Julie – outgoing, lively and living the dream. 'I used to call them the chipmunks, those two,' Simon later told *The Times*. 'Because from the second they opened their eyes they would talk. It made me laugh because I would wake up and I'd hear them talking.'

Gradually, the local movie-star glamour began to waft over the Cowells' fence and the family became part of the smart Elstree set. That other world Simon had seen being inhabited by his neighbours became *his* world. The crackle of laughter and the pop of champagne corks could now be heard in the Cowell household – and young Simon Cowell loved it.

Julie Cowell: 'We met lots and lots of famous people – Liz Taylor, Richard Burton and all the rest of them. We were all included in these parties. Of course Simon didn't realise how famous they were. Bette Davis used to ask him to sit on her knee.'

'Growing up in Elstree was amazing,' Simon later told his local paper, the *Borehamwood and Elstree Times*. 'It was like having a slice of Hollywood on your doorstep. If there's one thing I was taught, it was you have to work hard to get where you want to be, and that's exactly what I did.'

Indeed, so happy were those childhood days at Abbots Mead that there seem to be aspects of Cowell's personality today that appear to cling desperately to them – particularly his ongoing love affair with kids' food and pastimes. He loves to watch sixties' cartoons such as *The Flintstones* and *The Jetsons* rather than the news. Not for him the posh nosh available at the kinds of top-end restaurants he could so easily afford: Simon Cowell loves the food of his youth, the comfort-food staple that is beans on toast and the sticky, sweet simplicity of Angel Delight.

Despite these idyllic surroundings, in later life Simon would take great pleasure in pointing out what a brat he was as a child. 'A very strong character, believe you me' is how Julie Cowell described her son as a child to US talk-show host Larry King. 'I think he was about four years of age before I began to realise he had this great sort of strength in him. He wanted to do what he wanted to do and I'd have to pitch myself against him.'

He would be replacing his dad's handkerchief with a pair of frilly knickers, scratching his mum's Shirley Bassey records, taking up smoking courtesy of stolen cigarettes (Cowell is still an enthusiastic smoker), feeding red wine to half-brother Michael's dog or cutting brother Nicholas's hair down to the scalp. 'When Simon was five, I bought a new hat and asked him if I looked nice in it,' Julie Cowell told *Yours* magazine some 45 years later. 'He replied, "You look like a poodle ..."'

'Manners maketh the man' was the answer Cowell gave when asked by America's *TV Guide* asked what the best advice his mother had ever given him was. 'I obviously didn't follow that.'

'Aged 16, I recall a boyfriend ringing the house for me,' half-sister June remembered in 2007. 'Simon was only seven and yet he answered the phone and said, "Oh, June's waiting in her double bed for you!" He had the ability to say what others were thinking. He was always intuitive, even if it was embarrassing.'

By 1965, the Cowells were on the move again. Eric Cowell sold Abbots Mead to American-born film director Stanley Kubrick for a hefty profit. Film fans obsessed by his work treat it as something of a shrine. Many of his most notable movies – *2001: A Space Odyssey*, *A Clockwork Orange* and *Barry Lyndon* – were all created while Kubrick lived at Abbots Mead. Kubrick's daughter Vivian would later use the name Mead as a pseudonym when she wrote the music for her father's film *Full Metal Jacket*. Kubrick sold Abbots Mead in 1981 – the purchasers still live there to this day.

The Cowells, meanwhile, relocated to the even more upmarket village of Radlett, living in an early example of an American-style 'gated community'. It was here that Simon met the girl later identified as delivering his first real kiss when he was aged just nine. Now grown up and living in California, Tara McDonald-Smith contacted *American Idol* producers after spotting Simon on US TV and her call was put through to the pop entrepreneur on air. 'This is really you, Tara?' Cowell asked as Tara was put through during a telephone question-and-answer session that formed part of the American show in 2008. 'This literally was my first kiss – this was my first crush.'

'He'd taken me to the bottom of his garden,' Tara later told the *People* newspaper. At the time she was known as Tara Miller and lived in a property called Tudor House. 'It was very cute and it was very memorable. We were just kids. We didn't know what we were doing! We used to play spin the bottle ... and I got him a lot of the time. It was all good.'

Radlett was also where Cowell's moneymaking abilities first kicked in. If there were two things that Radlett wasn't short of, it was big cars and long lawns, so the young Simon set about knocking on doors to get work, offering to cut grass and wash cars for cash. 'The principle from my parents was that you live in the house rent-free, we pay for the holidays but, when we go on holiday, you should earn your own spending money,' Cowell told the *Observer* newspaper in 2007. 'I loved having my own money. In school holidays I would always apply for jobs, in warehouses, petrol stations or on a farm – I was always happier working than just mucking around.'

One aspect of his childhood that clearly didn't make him happy was school. Radlett Prep School – a good, old-fashioned, independent day school founded in 1935 – was where the young Simon found himself. Traditional and proud of it, the school was strong on discipline, maths and sport. 'I was terrible,' he would remember with a shudder, talking to the *Guardian* newspaper in 2009. 'I was always pretending to be ill and my favourite trick was getting a cup of tea in the morning and I used to put the tea on my head for about 30 seconds, and then I'd call my mum and dad and say, "I'm not feeling very well, Mum, can you feel my head?" And it would always be hot. And that's how I used to get off school, because I hated school.'

Much had been made of Cowell's dislike of the education system – he's something of a hero to those who believe that true entrepreneurs don't fit into rigid systems like schools. But Simon's distaste for education seems to go beyond the usual boyish search for ways to play truant, and seems to have genuinely distressed him. 'Sunday nights when I was at school were the most miserable evenings of my life,' he later explained in an interview with Piers Morgan in 2010. 'Seven o'clock, this ghastly religious programme would come on and the theme tune would mean that I've got to get ready now for tomorrow and Mum would say, "Do your homework." I used to have this sickening feeling in my stomach because I dreaded Monday so much.'

Eventually, Radlett began issuing ultimatums to Simon's parents: the boy either shapes up or ships out. He shipped out and was sent to Dover College in Kent as a boarder. *Non Recuso Laborem* is the school motto – meaning 'I

Can't Refuse the Task'. The motto may well have dated back to the school's foundation in 1871, but it was studiously ignored by Simon Cowell. 'I couldn't bear the discipline and the boredom,' he later told writer Lyn Barber. 'Every time I sat in a chemistry lesson I thought, "What am I doing this for?" I don't ever want to be in a job that involves a Bunsen burner.'

Cowell would pen dramatic, heart-wrenching letters to his parents, making sure they were in no doubt about his dislike of the school and whom he blamed for his misery. 'When he was at boarding school, he used to write a letter every week,' Julie Cowell later told US TV host Oprah Winfrey. ' "Dear Mum and Dad, I hope you're very happy in your warm centrally heated home. I am freezing. I have nothing to eat here." You'd weep if you'd read the letters.'

Simon's younger brother Nicholas was already at Dover and the pair were able to continue the troublemaking double act they'd perfected back at Abbots Mead. Nicholas's company was the only positive part of going to Dover as far as Cowell was concerned, and he made sure his parents were fully aware of how miserable he was and how much he resented being sent away in his letters home. In fact, Cowell found school so oppressive it made him feel like 'jumping off a bridge'.

'I used to get very anxious about going back to school after the holidays,' he told writer Rebecca Hardy in 2009. 'I can still remember that feeling in the pit of my stomach. I used to think, "Get me out of this prison as quickly as possible. I know how to read. I know how to add up. I know where America is. I just want to start work." '

During his trips home, Simon would have seen the new TV show that had caught the public's imagination. The concept behind the BBC's *Top Town* had come on since the 1960s: the brash, ITV, 1970s way of finding talent via the telly was *New Faces*, which hit our screens in 1973. A panel of experts would pass judgement on amateur talent with the aim of discovering a new star. Lenny Henry, Les Dennis and Michael Barrymore were among those who found fame by appearing on the show. But the real stars were often the panellists and their judgements. Most notorious was songwriter and producer Tony Hatch. Audiences were shocked at Hatch's blunt appraisals of the acts, making him a national hate figure. He was 'TV's Mr Nasty'. Hatch recently told the *Retro Sellers* website that Simon Cowell acknowledged the debt that shows like *Pop Idol* and *Britain's Got Talent* owed to *New Faces*. 'He said that to me – he said, "You started it all and we're all very grateful to you."'

Hatch would recall how the show dominated the schedules and that, if the acts weren't right for such a big show, it was his job to tell them: 'On *New Faces* in the seventies, there were only three terrestrial TV channels then and so we would get 16 to 17 million viewers at 7.30 on a Saturday evening. And I would say to these people, "You've just been given the greatest opportunity you ever could have had and you've just thrown it away. You're not ready and you're not right." '

Back at boarding school, Simon was busy refusing the task; he refused to knuckle down to either work or authority. At one stage he was handed a five-week suspension after being caught drinking in a local pub. The severity of the school ban wasn't just because of the boozing: he was chiefly being punished because of his point-blank refusal to name the boys who were with him. Eventually, Simon was put back a year for his rebellious ways. This had the unfortunate effect of putting him in the same class as brother Nicholas, doubling the trouble for their unfortunate teachers. Simon was, according to his Dover housemaster George Matthews, 'A miserable little devil. Simon refused to do anything that he didn't want to do himself – he was quite successful at that.'

Two Cowells in one class proved too much, with Simon describing the result as 'chaotic'. 'It got to the stage where the headmaster basically said, "Either one of them leaves this school or we're going to kick the two of them out," ' Simon later confessed to the *Sun*.

Simon would leave Dover with two GCE O levels – the precursor to today's GCSEs – and delight at finally being free of school. His jubilation was slightly confused by the fact that he had no idea what to do next – so he went back into education, attending technical college in Windsor, grinding out one more O level. His only other achievement at Windsor appears to have been losing his virginity in a drunken session with another student. Simon Cowell, the man who would later put so many other inexperienced young people under intense pressure, later described this first foray into sex as 'the most nerve-racking experience of my life'. He later detailed the experience in grim detail to *GQ* magazine: 'I lied and said I'd already lost my virginity to try to sound big. She hadn't lost hers either but admitted it. On the day we planned to have sex it was like going to the gallows. I hadn't a clue what I was doing. We went to the pub beforehand for a drink and I was forcing beer down my neck. I couldn't get enough of it to numb what I thought would be the most humiliating moment of my life. We went back and had a bath and she jumped out and said, "Simon, I'm ready." I remember lying there contemplating just ending it all there and then. I somehow got through it. I just wanted to get her out as quickly as possible so I could tell all my mates I had done it.'

On leaving college, Simon needed a job – for no other reason than to appease his workaholic dad Eric. What followed was Cowell's short-lived, somewhat half-hearted stab at operating in the real world. Sadly, none of his valiant attempts to live like the rest of us worked out too successfully, probably because he went out of his way to make sure they didn't.

First, there was an attempt to induct him into the family trade by teaching about the building industry on a training course. He lasted about an hour before demanding that his dad Eric drive him back home. Then there was his application for a position as a trainee manager at Tesco – the interview was terminated when the prospective boss objected to Cowell's jeans and showed him the door. Finally, there was the civil service – Cowell was informed he was the most unsuitable candidate the interview panel had ever seen, which he took as a compliment. It seems clear that Simon was sabotaging any effort at getting him to do a 'proper' job. 'I vowed that I'd find a job where I didn't have to wear a suit and play by the rules,' Simon later told the *Daily Mail*. 'So I did.'

As well as a disrespect for authority and a desire to do things the way he wanted to, there was one other aspect of Simon's character that seems to have been fairly well formed by this relatively early stage in his life: 'He said at 19 that he wouldn't get married,' his mum Julie told *Yours* magazine in 2009. 'I thought he might change his mind, but it doesn't look likely to happen.'

Determined to start making his own luck, Simon contacted a cousin who worked at Elstree studios. He managed to get him work as a runner – the lowest rung of the showbiz ladder. 'Runner is another term for slave,' he later told Fox News. 'But I loved it; I had a great time. I'd get on set at five in the morning, work till about ten at night – no money, but it was just a blast.'

For £15 a week, Simon did whatever he was asked on the set of the TV series *Return of the Saint*, starring Ian Ogilvy. There's even a plaque now at Elstree to mark this moment in showbiz history. It reads, 'Simon Cowell – music mogul and creator of television's *The X Factor* who began his career as a runner at Elstree film studios.' You'd think he'd have been grateful to the place where it all started. Not a bit of it: he managed to crash a car into a wall at Elstree in a teenage joyriding incident.

Legend has it that Simon also worked briefly on the set of Stanley Kubrick's psychological horror film *The*

Shining. Kubrick – who, as we've seen, earlier lived in the former Cowell home Abbots Mead – bought another hefty property in 1977, Childwickbury Manor near St Albans, not far from Radlett. *The Shining* is probably best known for the sequence where a crazed Jack Nicholson smashes down a door with an axe to get at screen wife Shelley Duvall. 'I remember him [Simon] saying he used to clean Jack Nicholson's axe between takes for the most famous scenes,' half-brother Tony later told the *Sun*. 'He took it very seriously and was very proud. It was so shiny you could see your face in it. It's a far cry from where he is now. I think the only thing he shines these days are his teeth.'

Cowell's dad Eric was by now quite the showbiz estate agent, thanks to the friends he'd made in and around Elstree. Entertainment company EMI had bought into the studios in 1969 and Eric did their property deals and was on the company's board of directors. It's often thought that it was thanks to his dad's connections with EMI that Simon first entered the record industry. It was, in fact, down to mum Julie.

Seeing how her son was enthused by working in the entertainment industry, she wrote to EMI Music Publishing to ask if there were any jobs available in their post room. Failed labourer, unsuitable civil servant and part-time film-set axe polisher did not, perhaps, add up to the greatest CV ever assembled, but it was enough to get him an interview. In the music world, Cowell's flip, laid-back attitude found more of a welcome than at Tesco, and he got the job.

His delight at getting a full-time position in showbiz was

slightly curtailed when he realised it wasn't quite the direct route to fame and riches he'd imagined. The post room was not the most inspiring of places to work. 'I remember him being horrified that there were two men there who had been doing the job for 20 years,' Julie later told the *Daily Mail*. 'He said to me, "This is just a stepping stone, Mum. I want more." '

TWO

THE BIGGEST ARSEHOLES IN THE MUSIC BUSINESS

Simon Cowell walked through the doors of EMI just as the company's most notorious new signings were being thrown out of them. The Sex Pistols had been signed to the label on a two-year deal after punk exploded across the country in 1976. EMI was seen as a rather dusty, old-fashioned record label and the Pistols had been signed to help freshen up that image. Unlike so many of his peers, the young Cowell just didn't get punk. Sounding like someone's dad rather than a teenager, he told friends it was just a din performed by people who couldn't play their instruments. Simon knew what he was talking about, of course: he'd tried this newfangled punk thing himself – and he didn't like it. 'I went to a very, very small Stranglers gig in this horrific venue and literally everyone was gobbing at each other,' he later shuddered during an interview with *NME*. 'That made me realise this was not for me.'

There was, however, one aspect of punk that did appeal: the way television played a vital part in its explosion. Few people had heard of punk or the Sex Pistols until they made front-page news in December 1976 after swearing at teatime on the Bill Grundy Thames Television show *Today*. The nation was appalled – even though the incident was shown only in London – and the Pistols were being seen as the most infamous band in Britain. They lasted only a matter of weeks before being chucked off EMI in the New Year with £40,000 in the back pocket of their manager, the late Malcolm McLaren. They would write a song about their short-lived experience with the company, called, perhaps unsurprisingly, 'EMI'. Cowell – whose musical tastes at the time were more along the middle-of-the-road lines of Fleetwood Mac and the Eagles – recalls being mightily impressed by the hype the Grundy incident created, calling it 'cynical and brilliant'.

The period of music history that was unfolding as Simon entered the industry was one of the busiest the UK would ever see. Despite his misgivings, punk would do Simon Cowell and the 1980s a great favour – music steered away from the album-dominated, adult-oriented scene of the 1970s towards a market dominated by singles and fun. Independent record labels began to pop up, aiming just to stick out a few singles rather than sign up acts on ten-album deals.

After punk came wave after wave of fashion-led music movements: new wave, mod, ska, New Romantics, electro pop, hi-NRG – it seemed to be out with the old and in with the new on a weekly basis. This was fantastic news for a music industry always on the lookout for a fresh angle to sell its products.

It would be while toiling away in the EMI post room for

15 quid a week that Simon Cowell would develop the thick skin that would help him shrug off the barrage of insults and criticisms he would receive over the next thirty years of his career. Not only was he on the very bottom rung of the ladder, but he was also regarded with suspicion thanks to dad Eric's place on the EMI board – two perfectly good reasons to treat him like dirt. The man who would later shock the world with his rudeness was himself taken aback by the way he was treated by anyone higher up the ladder than he was – which was in effect, everyone. He didn't care. Sorting post and pushing trolleys of mail across London may not have been the most challenging work ever, but at least he had a foot in the door.

Show business is full of tales of mail boys who get a shot at the big time after knocking on the right door, and the young Cowell saw no reason why this shouldn't happen to him. Sadly, it didn't, and 18 months down the line he began to lose heart, something that would happen a fair few times over the coming years. Indeed, what followed would be a period of great indecision in Cowell's life. He knew what he wanted but he didn't know how to get it. As a result, his employment at EMI would be something of a revolving-door affair, as he left and returned several times.

He started to look further afield than EMI. After getting knocked back for a job at Ariola Records (later part of Bertelsmann Music Group, or BMG, which Cowell would have so much success with), he decided he needed to earn some proper money and quit his post room job. Brother Nicholas was by now an estate agent and was on ten times the salary Simon was getting, so he turned to dad Eric and his seemingly endless Filofax of contacts. Eric came through for his son and got Simon a job at an estate agency. His first job was to open the post, so it didn't exactly prove to be a giant leap forward. Rather bizarrely, back at EMI, they hadn't seemed to have noticed that Simon had actually left. In his absence, his obvious ambition to get on within the company had paid off and he was offered a job in its international publishing division. He was able to tell the estate agency what they could do with their job and headed back into the music industry.

The job he returned to EMI to do would involve a skill that Simon still uses today: matching American songs and songwriters to British artists and getting them to tackle the tunes over here. This involved the hard slog of going through thousands of songs available on the EMI catalogue that may have had success in America but hadn't broken through in the UK. He then had to start knocking on the doors of other record labels, trying to get meetings with their artist and repertoire, or A&R, representatives. A&Rs are the people who represent and develop artists signed to their label. Simon Cowell's view of these vital cogs in the music industry was slightly different: he described them at the time as 'the biggest arseholes in the music business'.

But, from a standing start, Simon managed to start getting through the mire of record company politics and arseholes and was matching songs to artists at the rate of four or five a week. Flushed with this success, he figured that there clearly wasn't too much to this music-publishing malarkey, and in 1981 decided to quit EMI – again – and set up his own firm with colleague Ellis Rich, perhaps thinking that his new partner's surname was some kind of omen. Nearly 20 years older than Cowell, Rich had also started off as a post room boy and was experienced enough to have been involved in selling sheet music as well as having handled songs by the likes of Blondie and Queen.

The pair set up offices in London's Soho, using their first names as a company name – E&S Music. By the end of the first day Simon realised they had bitten off far more than they could chew. He swallowed his pride and went back to EMI yet again to ask for his old job back. Unsurprisingly, EMI told him he'd had his chance and blown it – he was going to have to make a go of E&S whether he liked it or not. Ellis Rich has since painted a far more positive image of how the pair got on in the venture. 'When I left EMI I took Simon Cowell with me,' Rich later told RMC TV. 'There was one point in our first year where we had five tracks in the Top 40 – Pointer Sisters, Boystown Gang – a nice selection of records and a good time was had by all.'

One good time that was had by Cowell at this time involved his dressing up as a canine superhero. It would often be claimed that the first and only time Cowell performed on a record was as Wonder Dog on the 1982 dance record 'Ruff Mix'. In fact, the man behind Wonder Dog was German synthesiser pioneer Harry Thumann, who was an early champion of the then new-fangled technique of 'sampling' sounds and electronically distorting them. In this case, take a dog's bark, make it go higher and lower and, bingo, you've got a 'tune'. With song titles such as 'Boney Boney' and 'Christmas Tail', Wonder Dog was hardly high art – just another in the long list of novelty records that had graced the British charts since they first began. It would be a list that Simon would add to many times over the next two decades.

When the Wonder Dog single 'Ruff Mix' started to take off in 1982, a willing volunteer was required to act as a stand-in to do the rounds of Saturday morning kids' shows that were the staple diet of the promotional process at that time. Armed only with a full-length dog costume and series of excruciating canine gags, Simon Cowell stepped into the breech and did the honours. 'He made up all these names like his friend Al Satian,' Ellis Rich later told Channel 5 (now Five). 'The whole thing was just a list of puns.'

Playing the part of Wonder Dog, he listed his musical influences as 'The Korgis and Bow Wow Wow', though he drew the line at Cat Stevens, as he was 'barking up the wrong tree'.

'Ruff Mix' reached Number 31 in the UK charts, high enough to warrant an appearance for Wonder Dog on *Top of the Pops*. The host of the show that night was Radio 1 DJ Peter Powell, the man who would later become Simon's agent.

Perhaps inspired by his canine capers as Wonder Dog, Simon began to go cold on the idea of music publishing, believing that actually making records was where his future belonged. Although E&S were making money, he was having a problem handling the rejections that inevitably came with the job. He and Ellis had jetted off to America and managed to secure meetings with top publishing companies in Los Angeles – who never rang them back.

Again, Simon Cowell found an experienced partner for his next venture – setting up a record label. Iain Burton's background was as a dancer, but by the early eighties he had gone into management, supplying dancers for pop videos and television shows. He had experienced huge success with the racy dance troupe Hot Gossip, whose choreographer was Arlene Phillips. Some 25 years later Phillips would be part of the BBC's *Strictly Come Dancing* show, which would rival Simon's *The X Factor* as a Saturday night ratings winner.

Hot Gossip had hit their peak in 1978, riding the disco craze with 'I Lost My Heart to a Starship Trooper'. It was sung by Sarah Brightman – later Mrs Andrew Lloyd Webber. By the early 1980s, Hot Gossip's appeal began to fade. They had undergone a variety of personnel changes and now included a teenage girl from Seattle called Sinitta Renet Malone, usually known just as Sinitta.

Burton and Cowell had decided to name their new label Fanfare – and the label's first single release would be Hot Gossip's 'Don't Beat Around the Bush'. It didn't chart, but it would prove to be a starting point for both Simon's later success with Fanfare and his extended relationship with Sinitta.

Sinitta had been living in London since she was a child and had proved herself a versatile performer. Whether she was on stage in *Cats* or writhing around as a backing dancer with the sexy soul trio Imagination on the TV show *The Tube* in 1982 (despite claiming she was born only in 1968) she clearly had ambition and ability. She also had a family history in music – her mum, Miquel Brown, was a singer and actress and, at the very time Simon was meeting Sinitta, Brown was scoring UK hits of her own with songs such as 'So Many Men, So Little Time' and 'He's a Saint, He's a Sinner'. Brown's brand of pumped-up electro-camp was from the hi-NRG school of music that included Boystown Gang, with whom Simon had scored hits as a publisher.

By this stage, Cowell needed to prove himself as someone who could discover and nurture talent as well as make money from matching up artists and songs. He decided Sinitta would be his first signing; by his own admission, he didn't know what he was doing, but the two got on so well that it would certainly be fun trying.

In Sinitta, Simon had an artist who could sing and dance and looked the part; what the would-be Svengali now needed was a song. He asked songwriter and producer George Hargreaves – whom he'd met at EMI – if he had anything suitable. Hargreaves was in the throes of writing a new song that had come to him after he had been working with the singer Princess. She'd ad-libbed a line during a recent recording session in which she'd described someone as being 'so macho'. 'I heard Princess sing those words and I thought: that's my next song,' Hargreaves later told the *Scotsman* newspaper. 'I wrote it that same evening. It was a caricature of the medallion man. It was for women to dance round their handbags to and for the gay scene to go mad to on poppers.'

Hargreaves – to say the least a colourful character – later became a fundamental Christian and used the money he earned from the song to fund his religious and political ambitions to be a Euro MP.

His opponents made great capital of the fact that the man behind such a gay disco classic would later campaign that homosexuality was a sin. 'It says in the Bible that so long as Earth remains there shall be seed time and harvest,' he later said, by way of an elaborate explanation. 'You could say that "So Macho" was the seed I sowed and now I'm reaping the harvest.'

'So Macho' certainly proved to be manna from heaven for Simon and Sinitta – but it took time. The record initially stalled at Number 40 in the charts and would need to be re-released twice more before it finally took off and peaked at Number 2. The super-cheesy video to accompany it – featuring Sinitta as a psychiatrist's patient – was shot for £2,000. The hit saved Simon's job, launched his career and stopped Fanfare from closing down after Simon's partner Iain Burton began having second thoughts about the viability of the label.

As they worked to further Sinitta's career, the teenager and her boss became closer and closer. The young singer also became very friendly with Simon's parents, even living at their house for a time. But Sinitta would later paint a devastating picture of Cowell's behaviour towards her during the 1980s. In an interview she gave to the *People* in August 2003, she described a relationship in which sex was nonexistent.

'It didn't feel right,' she said of the night that Cowell first initiated sex with her. 'I don't think he ever forgave me. I was always trying to attract him but he never laid a hand on me again.'

She went on to describe how Cowell would tell her that

he didn't find her sexually attractive and would tell her he was sleeping with her friends. 'I walked into our bedroom and he was there in bed with two blonde girls and they were all naked,' Sinitta said. 'They were quite ugly and quite fat; I couldn't understand what he would see in girls like that ... they were in my bed doing this.'

The interview has since come back to haunt both Cowell and Sinitta and their reactions to it have been very different. Simon's response when the issue is raised is a very Cowell-esque dismissal. 'Oh, people say things,' he told the *Daily Mail,* batting the issue away. 'If I thought they really meant them – well, let's just say that Sinitta is genuinely one of the most important people in my life, and always will be.'

When the same interview is quoted back at Sinitta, her reaction now is bafflement: 'We did have a proper physical relationship,' she later claimed in an interview with writer Natalie Clarke. 'I don't know how this idea we didn't has come about. We didn't at first, because I was underage; but later on, yes, absolutely.'

When Simon and Sinitta did finally split up, Simon was far more heartbroken about the separation than he let people think, according to his half-brother Michael. 'When they split it was actually the first time you could tell he was genuinely upset about a girl,' Michael later told the *Mirror.* 'It hit him really hard. I met Sinitta several times. She was beautiful. She was one of the family. Mother loved her. I would go over for Sunday lunch and she would be there. She was very chatty and good fun. Everyone was upset when it ended.'

To cheer himself up, Simon went on a 'lads' holiday' in Majorca and invited his half-brother along, something Michael would later regret: 'We we were in lap-dancing clubs. We were drinking, smoking, meeting women. I had never really been involved in this life before. Simon was really very wealthy already and was leading the high life. We met lots of women and drank cocktails. The memory is hazy but we had a great time. I was a respectable married man and when I got back to the UK my wife found out about it. We ended up getting divorced.'

By this time another key player had entered Simon's life. Initially, his relationship with her would be short to the point of being virtually nonexistent – but it would create another unbreakable friendship. Jackie St Clair, also known as Jackie Marinetti, managed to develop quite a racy tabloid profile in the eighties and nineties, with her name being romantically linked to famous names including pop star Prince, the Duke of Northumberland and Andrew Ridgeley of Wham!. A regular Page Three girl for the *Sun* and a former Miss Nude UK, she had also appeared in men's top-shelf magazines. Indeed her association with Ridgeley allowed *Oui* magazine to run a naked centrefold of her under the headline WHAM! BAM! THANK YOU MA'M! If you look up the expression 'sultry brunette' in the dictionary, there is a picture of Jackie St Clair. Or at least, there should be …

Despite her high profile, St Clair has always been a model of discretion when it comes to her friendship with Simon Cowell. She now lives next door to his London home. In turn, Simon has painted a picture of St Clair as a woman who lived on 'the other side of the fence' like the glamorous folk he saw as a kid back in Elstree. Confident, worldly, vivacious – and, essentially, way out of his league. When they met she operated a policy of 'treat 'em mean to keep 'em keen', and Cowell admits he fell for her big time. Their physical relationship seems to have been replaced by a strong friendship that baffles outsiders. The mystery has added spice to the Simon/Sinitta/St Clair story that it would otherwise lack. Whatever the true nature of the bond is, there's no denying it's a strong one. 'Sinitta and Jackie are my family now,' Cowell recently told the *Mirror*. 'I don't think of them as ex-girlfriends any more. They are an extension of my life ... It must be infuriating, but I'd never change because my ex-girlfriends are so close I couldn't imagine life without them.'

Back at Fanfare, Simon was doing the sums for 'So Macho': they'd turned an outlay of just a few grand for studio time and a cheap-as-chips video into a million-pound hit. Easy. But a follow-up would prove elusive – Sinitta's next release six months later was 'Feels Like the First Time', and it scraped only to Number 45. If he was to secure a future for the label and for Sinitta, Simon would need more songs that were as ludicrously catchy as 'So Macho' – and he would need a mentor to help guide him.

Enter former Mecca club DJ, ex-manager of the ska band The Specials, one time A&R man and now a record producer, Coventry-born Pete Waterman, whose CV made Cowell's look very slight indeed. By 1984 he had started producing hits under the Stock Aitken Waterman (SAW) banner with Mike Stock and Matt Aitken. Again it would be the hi-NRG style that would reap them rewards, with hits often moulded out of what would at first seem to be unpromising raw materials.

After modest success with varied artists such as the cross-dressing actor Glenn Milstead (better known as Divine) and former Eurovision Song Contest hopeful Hazell Dean, SAW hit gold in December 1984 with Dead or Alive's 'You Spin Me Round (Like a Record)', somehow turning gobby Liverpool punk Pete Burns into a *bona fide* pop star.

As blunt as a lump hammer, Waterman was a man who had never knowingly shown the world his modest side; Cowell believed him to be a genius. Simon wanted him on board and employed a technique he would use repeatedly over the years – harassment. 'He used to follow me everywhere,' Waterman told Trevor McDonald in 2007. 'Literally, I'd turn round and there was Simon. He used to pester me like mad to work with him. But it was always obvious Simon had got ... *it*. He wouldn't be deflected. What I liked about Simon was his energy and his drive. His determination was phenomenal. If you are a record producer or a songwriter you need someone to sell your record – and there wasn't anyone better at selling a record than Simon Cowell. Nobody.'

But Waterman hasn't always been quite so complimentary about Simon Cowell. The older man's bluff manner and no-nonsense approach clearly struck a chord with Simon, and he seems to have used Waterman as something of a role model: This is how a music-biz mogul acts – I'll copy him. 'If I'm ever cruel,' Simon reasoned in an interview with the *Daily Mail*, 'It's because show business is cruel. But I learned much over the years, from people like Pete Waterman – real tough love. He once said to me, "You don't know what you're talking about. You're bloody useless. Come back when you've got a hit." I took it as a challenge.'

The song that Simon harassed from the SAW team was 'Toy Boy'. It featured a girlie rap and a chorus catchier than swine flu. They even splashed out on a proper video this time around. Given that Sinitta was only just out of her teens herself when the promo film was shot, schoolboy model Felix Howard – best known for appearing in Madonna's 'Open Your Heart' video – was cast as her 'love interest'. The song also set something of a template for SAW: listen to it alongside the following year's 'I Should Be So Lucky' by Kylie Minogue, and you will see how unwilling the team had become to change a winning formula. Although 'Toy Boy' reached only Number 4 in the UK charts, it sold well across worldwide markets. To many, 'Toy Boy' is the quintessential piece of eighties pop fluff; Simon Cowell believes it's the song that made people take him and Fanfare seriously.

In fact, Simon was taking himself pretty seriously by this stage. He had the lot: the job, the looks, the Porsche, the posh pad in Fulham. He was, by his own admission, a 'walking, talking eighties cliché'. Perhaps to bring him back down to earth, his brothers hatched a plan to let Simon know what they thought he was in danger of turning into. While he was on holiday they redecorated the front of his home to look like a Chinese restaurant, complete with sign over the door. When he returned, Simon was greeted to the sight of an establishment called the 'Wan Kin'.

'It was a time where everything was gonna be great – a real sense of optimism, greed is good,' he confessed twenty years later to the *Mirror*. 'You have a Porsche. You should have a Chelsea house. I was very much part of that. I wasn't earning enough to sustain that kind of lifestyle and I was borrowing a lot of money from the bank to buy shares which I was told would quadruple over a period of time.'

However, in true 1980s fashion, after the boom came the bust. Cowell was living beyond his means and, despite the success he was having, there was more going out than coming in. When the parent of his record company Fanfare went bust, shares that Simon had ploughed his money into went too. He was teetering on the edge of bankruptcy and owed the bank almost £400,000; everything had to go. He admitted to the *Daily Mail* that he had nobody to blame but himself: 'I lived this life of excess: out every night, partying. I had all the material stuff – the big house, flash cars – but all of it had been bought on credit. None of it was really mine. On one level, going bust didn't bother me. It was the eighties, and there wasn't the stigma about bankruptcy that you might think. My mates weren't bothered. My dad was in business – he knew that it happened, too. He loaned me the money to bail me out, and I got a loan from the bank to pay him back. It was £1,000 a month, I seem to remember.'

He spent the last few pounds he had on a taxi to his

parents' home. With their children now grown up, Eric and Julie Cowell lived in an apartment in London and Simon moved back in with them to lick his wounds. 'It was shattering for him to have to move back in with his parents again at the age of 30-something,' Julie told ITV twenty years later. 'He never ever felt sorry for himself; he was determined to do something about it. And he did.'

Cowell recalls that his mum was delighted to have him back home. And dad Eric didn't preach to or criticise his son. He just told him to start from scratch – and this time do it properly. 'In a way it was exciting to start all over again because I did it on such different terms,' Cowell said. 'Every penny I earned was, well, mine – and no one was going to take it away again. It made life so much sweeter.'

The old Simon Cowell – the indecisive one who knew what he wanted but couldn't work out how to get it – was gone. The new Simon Cowell – the one who'd flown too close to the sun and had his wings scorched – would do things very differently. And he'd change the world.

THREE
MY BEST FRIEND

If money had been an issue for Simon Cowell, then the £80 cash and the set of kitchen utensils he won on TV's *Sale of the Century* show in 1990 must surely have come in handy. Cowell's appearance on the show – it had moved to satellite TV by this stage and original host Nicholas Parsons was long gone – is now a favourite of *Before They Were Famous*-style television clip shows. Fellow contestant Barbara Humphreys recalled, 'Watching the video now I remember thinking Simon was quite posh and handsome. He had a good sense of humour, but I would never have put him down as a future superstar.'

Apart from the distraction of his teeth being a normal, non-radioactive shade of white, the main surprise when viewing the clip today is how well he comes across as a contestant. Described as a 'record company director from London who's a keen go-kart racer', he is charming and self-deprecating; he takes it seriously (but not too seriously) and deserves to win. Unfortunately, some other people in his immediate circle were meanwhile not doing quite as well.

As a quintessential eighties artist, Sinitta would discover that the new decade was not so kind in UK chart terms. 'Hitchin' a Ride' was her first release of the nineties and it managed to get only to Number 24. Follow-up 'Love and Affection' only managed Number 62. The party decade was over and Simon Cowell would need other ways to keep the hits – and the cash – coming.

By 1989 Simon Cowell had been poached from his job at Fanfare to become one of the 'biggest arseholes in the music business' – an A&R man. His new employer was BMG. The company had been distributing Fanfare's records and was a major player compared with Simon's tiny indie. There was a catch to the job though: Simon would not only have to discover new talent, he would also have to guarantee they sold records – a lot of records. If his acts failed to hit minimum sales targets, he'd be out.

At the time, house music was king. The thunderous beats and simple melodies were everywhere – and, as with punk, Simon just didn't get it. Anything too dancy and up-tempo seemed to baffle him. When he was offered the chance to sign a five-man act from the Mecca of the new dance vibe, Manchester, he passed. 'I was shown a picture by the manager Nigel Martin-Smith and I remember saying at the time, "I'll sign them if you dump the fat one" ... Gary Barlow. He was overweight at the time with a weird haircut. Obviously I made a huge mistake.'

The signings he did make were hardly great leaps of the imagination; at the risk of sounding a little harsh, some might have been said to have been a little past their sell-by dates. It looked as if Cowell was playing it safe.

At the age of 18 Sonia Evans had gone to Number 1 in the UK with her debut single 'You'll Never Stop Me From Loving You', a classic slice of Stock Aitken Waterman disco cheese complete with budget video. The song made her the youngest female to hit the top spot since Mary Hopkin ('Those Were the Days') in 1968. Tiny, red-haired and bubbly to the point of being annoying, Sonia had famously attracted Pete Waterman's attention by hanging around outside his recording studio and singing at him – but by the start of the nineties she had left the SAW camp and would never again make the Top 10 as a solo artist. Despite this, Cowell signed her and sent her down the cover-version route with a rendering of Heatwave's 1977 disco hit 'Boogie Nights'. It just made the Top 30. Next was 'Better the Devil You Know' – not a patch on the SAW Kylie Minogue song of the same name – as it was the UK entry in the 1993 Eurovision Song Contest. With that much TV exposure, Cowell reasoned the song couldn't fail. Sonia came second in the competition and managed to get to 15 in the UK charts. Good – but not great.

Next there was Curiosity. Formally known as Curiosity Killed the Cat, they had been the hippest thing in town with their jazzy brand of pop funk and their loose-limbed pin-up lead singer Ben Volpeliere-Pierrot. Their early singles were finger-snapping fun with an arty edge – they even managed to get pop art giant Andy Warhol to appear in the video for their debut 'Misfit'. Sadly, all that was in 1986. By start of the 1990s they'd been dropped by

Mercury records after diminishing sales returns. So it was a surprise to see them back three years later with a slimmed-down name signed by Simon to RCA. At first, things went well with a cover of Johnny Bristol's hit 'Hang On In There Baby' going Top Three and spending a healthy 10 weeks in the UK charts. But the two follow-ups fared badly – 'I Need Your Lovin'' just managed a Top 50 place and 'Gimme the Sunshine' barely scraped the Top 75.

It was Top 10 or nothing for Simon Cowell – he was in effect breaking the terms of his BMG deal. It must have really rubbed him up the wrong way to see the middling successes he was having, just as the band he rejected with the fat lead singer – Take That – were conquering all before them. Simon had to sell records at all costs. His 'new' acts weren't delivering, so he had to change tactics to survive. He needed something new and the wait was getting frustrating. Cowell recalled this period in an interview with journalist Ariel Leve in 2005. 'A man named Mike McCormack [RCA executive] sat with me and said, "Let me give you a piece of advice. You are the musical equivalent of Gary Lineker. What you do is stand by the goal. When the right thing comes along, nod it in the back of the net. Something's going to come along." He trusted me, and it helped to clear my mind. Then you realise that the reason things had gone badly before wasn't the people I was working with: it was my fault. I just wasn't getting it together. I stopped blaming everyone else.'

He drew on everything he'd learnt so far – from Elvis and Colonel Tom Parker to Sinitta's success on MTV with her cheap and cheerful videos – and found a link. It wasn't the trendy music press or the radio DJs who sold records: it was television. Being at the cutting edge didn't matter so long as your act was seen on the small screen. The new talent he began scouting for wouldn't be found in a dingy club or a music venue – it was right there in his living room already. 'From about the age of 30 I was fascinated with the influence television had on people,' he recalled in an interview with Fox News. 'Most of my peers were signing worthy rock acts, tortured artists, alternative groups, and I was just interested in volume – that's all I was interested in. And I realised that television was having an amazing, enormous influence on people and I started to sign things like the wrestlers from the World Wrestling Federation.'

Wrestling had come a long way since the 1970s, when it was a staple of the schedule on as part of ITV's *World of Sport* on Saturday afternoons. The grunt-and-groan game and its UK stars such as Big Daddy and Giant Haystacks had given way to their bigger, brasher and brighter American counterparts courtesy of the World Wrestling Federation (WWF). As the US version took off in Britain, thanks to exposure on satellite TV, the wrestling stars began selling out the kind of British arenas that many music stars could only dream of. Cowell reasoned that, if fans were willing to shell out for a ticket, a T-shirt and a novelty foam hand, there was no reason why they wouldn't go one further and buy a record too. He was right, but it was hardly a new idea. In truth, the WWF had been releasing albums in the US since the mid-eighties. *The Wrestling Album*, released in 1985, featured the introduction music used by stars such as Hulk Hogan and Rowdy Roddy Piper. What Cowell did was adapt the idea for the UK market. 'I remember when I went to my immediate boss and told her that we were going to sign the WWF wrestlers,' Cowell would later explain to *Rolling Stone* magazine. 'She just paled and said, "Who on earth is going to buy records from wrestlers?" She honestly thought I was just a freak. But my attitude was simple: I don't care what we're selling, as long as we're selling records.'

That's exactly what Cowell started to do. He sold records – lots of records – but without the need for airplay or glowing reviews. It didn't go down well with the critics or the snootier side of BMG, but that hardly gave him sleepless nights. 'We sold a million, million and a half records,' he later told America's *60 Minutes* show when recalling his success with the WWF. 'I couldn't care less – it's a business. I'm sure a three-star Michelin chef is looking at the people who are making McDonald's hamburgers and saying, "These people are terrible." But I'd rather be McDonald's than the three-star Michelin chef. Genuinely I would.'

The next act in his sights were TV puppets Zig and Zag from the planet Zog. The furry stars of Channel 4's *The Big Breakfast* were twins from outer space with bizarre growths on the tops of their heads and heavy Irish accents – Simon would come across something along very similar lines years later on *The X Factor*.

Then there were the Mighty Morph'n Power Rangers, stars of the martial-arts TV show that had taken the country by storm. His desire to sign these acts would cause major friction with colleagues at BMG. 'I was hard done by,' he revealed in an interview with *The Times*. 'The records weren't selling the way I wanted, I had a small team around me who would have agreed with basically anything I said, and it got to a point where I walked out and went to see the chairman of the company. I told him, "I'm going to leave."'

Simon was transferred to sister label RCA and took Zig and Zag and the Power Rangers with him. By December 1994 Cowell had both acts nestled in the UK Top Three and an extremely smug look on his face. He didn't care what colleagues or critics thought – he'd delivered. 'I'm only ashamed or embarrassed if I spend my money, or my company's money, on something which is a flop,' he would reflect in an interview with the *Mirror*. 'How could I possibly be ashamed of making a record which 500,000 have enjoyed?'

Simon had developed a method he maintains to this day: knowing what the public want before they do and giving it to them. 'I realised that the record was just an extension of the other merchandise available and it became my specialist area, really,' he revealed on America's Fox News. 'And even though I knew at the time these weren't long-term artists, obviously – but I thought, It's a learning curve, and I always used to call that period target practice. And I always believed that there was something bigger down the line from this.'

There was devastating news in the offing for the Cowell family at this time. In 1995 Simon's beloved mum Julie was diagnosed with breast cancer. The family rallied round but after surgery to remove the malignant lump, she refused to let her husband or her sons accompany her to hospital as she endured six weeks of radiotherapy. 'I had to do it alone,' she later told the *Daily Mail*. 'My boys would come and see me, and mostly I could say hand on heart that I was fine. But I didn't want to risk them seeing me at a low moment because it would have worried them. As a mother, your first role is to protect your children. On the day I got the all-clear, Simon sent me a bunch of flowers so big that I couldn't get them through the door.'

Despite a further scare, when there were fears that the cancer had spread to her lung, the formidable Julie Cowell would make a full recovery.

Away from the strains and stresses of the real world, Simon's next TV-related success would make his previous forays into the worlds of furry aliens and Lycra-clad martial artists seem pretty small beer. It would also make them seem positively credible in the eyes of his critics. Actors Robson Green and Jerome Flynn were familiar small-screen faces, thanks to their roles as Fusilier Dave Tucker and Sergeant Paddy Garvey in the ITV army series *Soldier Soldier*. During one episode the pair were seen to take a swipe at 'Unchained Melody'. The song had been around since the mid-1950s but it had been the 1965 version by The Righteous Brothers that had made the tune a standard.

Simon believed that the pair could have a hit if they released their version, but the actors weren't interested. So he resorted to a tried-and-tested technique: harassment. 'It got to the point where Robson's lawyer phoned me and said, "If you harass my client any more we are going to take a restraining order against you," ' he said on TV's *This Is Your Life*. 'I thought, Sod it, I'll start on the mother and eventually his mother persuaded them to make the record. And they sold seven or eight million albums in two years – it was fantastic.'

'Unchained Melody' went to Number 1 in May 1995 and spent 17 weeks in the chart. It would be Simon's first Number 1 and the first of three in a row for Robson and Jerome. Despite the damning reviews and the way the two actors would look at each other while singing, the money started flooding in. There would be another advantage for Robson Green of working with Simon: he got to meet Cowell's personal assistant Vanya Seager. A former model and Bond girl – she had a bit part in *For Your Eyes Only* – Vanya was a dark-haired beauty in the Jackie St Clair mould. She and Green are now married but at the time they kept their relationship a secret from Cowell, with Green adopting a variety of fake voices to phone her at the RCA offices. 'Simon was devastated when I nicked her,' Green later confessed to the *Mirror*. 'He's never forgiven me.'

It's true to say not everyone fell for Robson and Jerome's charms. When the pair appeared on *Top of the Pops*, one audience member went to the trouble of wearing a T-shirt with the slogan 'Robson and Jerome are a Load of Old Bollocks' emblazoned across it. Manchester rockers Oasis also failed to sign up to the singing actors' fan club – they were furious when Robson and Jerome's second single, 'I Believe', kept their song 'Wonderwall' from the top slot in November. The Gallaghers could rest easy though, because after two albums Robson and Jerome called it a day – despite having a £3 million cheque wafted under their noses to make a third. Their success was one of the more baffling musical stories of the nineties – compilations albums of their greatest hits still sell well, but to critics the two actors became a byword for all that was wrong with the music industry.

It's also true that not every actor who thought he had musical talent was necessarily right. Simon signed *Baywatch* star David Hasselhoff on the basis that he was the biggest thing on the box and he was selling shedloads of records in Germany. Hasselhoff had managed an almost accidental Number 1 when his song 'Looking for Freedom' struck a chord with German record buyers as an unlikely anthem for the destruction of the Berlin Wall. Sadly, Simon didn't take into account the fickleness of the viewing public and the dubious musical tastes of German record buyers – the Hoff's 1993 single 'If I Could Only Say Goodbye' got to only 35 in the charts in the UK. Despite being alarmed by Hasselhoff's eccentric behaviour – he once pulled out a ghetto blaster in a restaurant and sang a song at full tilt into Simon's face to prove his talent – Cowell clearly developed a soft spot for him. 'He's larger than life and he's unpredictable, very emotional and funny,' Cowell said in an interview with US website *Monsters and Critics*. 'There's only one David Hasselhoff. I adore him.'

That's more than can be said for another actor who caught Cowell's eye around this time: Eddie Murphy. The *Beverly Hills Cop* star was in Cowell's sights after he heard Murphy was keen to make a music album. Action star

Bruce Willis had done good business in the UK charts, so why not Murphy? The answer became obvious when Cowell went to the US to listen to some tracks the actor had already recorded. They were, in Cowell's opinion, 'crap'. Unfortunately, the Cowell directness that the world knows today wasn't fully formed at this stage and Simon didn't have the nerve to tell Murphy what he really thought of the tracks. 'I flew to the east coast to his huge house, and I was very intimidated,' Simon would later tell the *Sun*. 'I thought it would be just the two of us and a hi-fi. But I ended up in a recording studio with about 20 nodders – a nodder is someone who gets paid to agree with the person paying him. Eddie started to play some songs – which I hated – and I just didn't know what to say. Now I'd find it a lot easier. I would just say – I hate it.'

Simon diplomatically offered to bring Murphy to the UK and record some fresh material – until he got his calculator out. He cancelled the deal when he realised that shipping Murphy and his entourage of nodders would set him back half a million quid before the star had even opened his mouth.

A far better investment was the 25 grand that Simon spent putting together boy band Five – or 5ive, as they were originally known. He commissioned the group after a gaffe even bigger than missing out on Take That, and that was letting the Spice Girls slip through his fingers. Cowell was one of several BMG A&R men circling the group. He claims he was on the trail of the five-piece girl band even before Simon Fuller, the man who eventually became their manager and later Simon's collaborator on *Pop Idol*.

Cowell was a day late making his offer – their debut single 'Wannabe' came charging out of the gates three months later in June 1996.

In response Simon paid Chris Herbert – who, with his father Bob had originally brought the five Spice Girls together – to do the same again, but with boys. This tactic would be another one to add to the Cowell arsenal for future reference: If first you miss out on something, create your own version of it. The point of Five was that they were the Spice Girls – but boys. They were even recruited the same way as the Spice Girls were – via an advert in the showbiz newspaper *The Stage*, which asked for boys with 'attitude and edge'. Despite their origins in the pages of *The Stage*, Five did indeed have a harder, streetwise image – a bit of rough compared with some of their softer contemporaries. Their debut single 'Slam Dunk (Da Funk)' got to Number 10 in December 1997 – the first of 11 Top Ten singles for the group. They managed three Number 1s among this tally, including the peerless dance floor filler 'Keep on Movin' '. Perhaps they'd have had four if they had recorded a song Simon was hoping to secure for the group: it was called 'Baby One More Time' and, despite his offering the song's writer Max Martin a Mercedes 600SL, the tune went to a new singer called Britney Spears. Martin did eventually write another pop gem for Five, but they refused to record it. It was called 'Bye Bye Bye' and *NSYNC made the second-hand song a hit across the world. Five could be a real handful for Simon.

There were no such problems for his other big signing

of 1997 – there was barely a cross word from any of this lot. In fact there were barely any identifiable words to be heard at all from the Teletubbies. The preschool sensations were the big TV hit of the year and a single was sure to be a hit – and that's when the A&R men come out to play. 'I heard another record label were about to sign the Teletubbies,' Simon later boasted to the *Sun*. 'So I got the BBC in my office and told them I would give them £500,000 in advance. We knew a record like that would make over £2 million.' 'Teletubbies Say Eh-Oh' duly went to Number 1 and stayed in the charts for a tubbie-tastic 32 weeks. It would be the last truly great Simon Cowell kids' TV hit single.

The Teletubbies and his other musical creations would be constantly used as sticks to beat Cowell with in years to come: why should anyone listen to the musical opinion of the man behind the Teletubbies? His critics would make the mistake of confusing Simon Cowell with a man who cared about their opinion. 'My definition of credibility,' he would patiently explain to *The Times*, 'is public acceptance. Record sales.'

To push that point home, Simon's final big deal of the decade would be his biggest. A call from Irish pop manager Louis Walsh in June 1998 persuaded Cowell to fly to Dublin. Walsh – the former manager of Ireland's triple Eurovision winner Johnny Logan – had been pestering Cowell for years: 'Louis used to call me over and over and over again,' Simon said in the documentary *In My Life*. 'I had no idea who he was. Three or four times a week my PA would say, "This guy from Ireland's on the phone, Louis

Walsh, will you talk to him?" "No." But he was the most persistent person I'd ever met in my life.'

Eventually the pair did meet, backstage at a TV show in Dublin in the Robson and Jerome days. Cowell claims Walsh was 'dribbling with excitement' at finally coming to face to face with him. Since then Louis had become a genuine player, as he'd put together Boyzone, the so-called 'Irish Take That'. The group had managed great success through the 1990s but by the end of the decade their star was fading as lead singer Ronan Keating was preparing to go solo. Walsh was looking for something new. He'd spotted an embryonic boy band called IOYOU on the Irish TV show *Nationwide* and wanted them to audition for Cowell.

Simon walked into the Westbury Hotel in Dublin that day and saw what he later described as 'one of the worst looking boy bands I have ever seen in my life'. One of the lads – Shane Filan – was not at his best, having taken the decision to get beered up the night before. Shane painted a vivid picture of what happened next in the band's autobiography *Our Story*, describing Simon as 'a man with black hair and really high-waisted black trousers'.

'He wasn't famous at all at this stage,' Shane said. 'He was just a successful A&R man. His big band of the time was Five, so we knew he would be great to work with. I performed terribly. The rest of the lads were great, but I knew I hadn't done my job. Simon seemed unimpressed ... as I came out of the audition room Louis grabbed me and kinda half hit me.'

Cowell turned them down flat and advised Walsh to get

some new members. A second audition was organised with an amended line-up, but Walsh still had faith in the boozy talents of Filan. So he got the singer to dye his hair and get a tan to fool Cowell into thinking Shane had been given the boot. Band member Kian Egan: 'Shane's hair was longer and blond as per Louis's cunning plan and he'd been on a couple of sun beds, so he was browner. As we were just about to start, Simon pointed at Shane and said to Louis – I swear to God – "Who's the new guy?" '

'Second time I saw them it was a different band,' Simon said. 'They'd got some new people in. They just *had* it. They were confident this time, great song choices … just what the market needed. I instantly got it and I didn't fool around with him, I said, "Louis I'm going to my lawyers now, we have a deal." '

Simon signed the band but insisted they change their name to Westside – later to become Westlife when other bands were found already using the name. Simon tied them to a five-album deal. The group – Shane and Kian along with Nicky Byrne, Mark Feehily and Brian McFadden – went to Cowell's offices in London to put pen to paper. It would be the first of many visits to Cowell's lair over the years. One thing would tickle them: they couldn't help but notice that Cowell had a giant mirror behind his desk engraved with the words 'Yes Simon, you do look terrific'.

Straight away Cowell was impressed by the Westlifers' work ethic. The Irishmen were ambitious and focused. Westlife *really* wanted it. 'They'd watched bands like Five and A1 come and go, so they didn't want to be like those bands,' Louis Walsh later told UTV. 'They wanted to be like Take That and live for ever.'

Their first single was to be the piano-led ballad 'Swear It Again', written by proven British hit makers Steve Mac and Wayne Hector. Cowell's dad Eric loved the track and predicted it would go to the top of the charts. Simon was totally focused on the song, even scrapping a £150,000 video and starting from scratch because he felt it wasn't perfect. He knew this was his chance to break away from the novelty records and start having some real hits.

Westlife were on the covers of all the glossy pop mags – highly unusual for a band who didn't even have a record out – and by April 1999 were bracing themselves for a hefty hit. They were in Pete Waterman's studio putting the finishing touches to their debut album when they got the news they had fulfilled Eric Cowell's prediction and topped the charts. Simon was on the other side of the world: 'The day Westlife got to Number 1, I was in America,' Simon later told the *Mirror*. 'I rang my mother to tell her. She sounded odd but I put the phone down and didn't think too much about it. Then half an hour later my brother Nicholas rang. He said: "Dad died this morning. Mum's in a state of shock and she said: 'I didn't want to tell Simon and ruin his day.' " '

Family friend Father Martin Morgan would later relive the events of that day on ITV's *This Is Your Life*. 'Simon was flying to Boston as Westlife had become Number 1. Eric died. I remember being with the family the next morning and there was a big debate about whether they should spoil Simon's success by telling him about his father's death. I persuaded them to ring him. I thought he'd always put family before the business. Certainly he put his father much higher than the business.'

Eric Cowell had died of a heart attack. Simon's raffish role model was gone. Simon returned to the UK, doing his grieving on the 14-hour flight home. The plane was delayed but he didn't mind – the longer the flight took the more time he had to compose himself. No one is prepared for the loss of a parent – but Simon Cowell has since admitted that he was particularly ill-equipped. 'I was living life like in one of those Disney movies, where I genuinely believed nobody was ever going to die,' he later revealed in an interview with the *Daily Mail*. 'When it happened, it was just the worst sense of reality I've ever felt in my life. Ever. So, yes, I cried, but I don't cry easily.'

The decade when Simon really broke through and achieved major success was made possible after his dad had taken his son back under his roof after nearly going bust. Eric Cowell had given Simon a blueprint for the way a life should be led – with fun and a sense of style. Now he was no longer there to show his son the way. Simon took a week off work and retreated from the world of show business. On his return 'Swear It Again' was still at Number 1. 'He had a fantastic ear for music, my dad,' Simon would later recall. 'I played him this song and he said, "They'll go to Number 1." The horrible irony attached to that ... He was my best friend and he gave me so much good advice. I'll never forget that.'

FOUR

'I WANT POPSTARS OFF THE MARKET'

After Westlife secured their first Number 1, 1999 saw Simon and Louis Walsh mount a devastating assault on the British charts. 'If I Let You Go' was next off the production line, a mid-paced number in a Backstreet Boys style. Simon had sent Westlife to Sweden to work at the Cheiron hit factory in Stockholm, which had been responsible for hits by *NSYNC, Backstreet Boys and Britney Spears, so it was no surprise their second hit had the pop sheen of the moment. By this stage the group were worthy of a trip to Tenerife to shoot the video. The song, combined with that Cheiron production and the sight of the lads striding through the surf in slow motion, was enough to take the record to the top slot.

Simon already a song in the bag for their third release: 'Flying Without Wings' – written by Steve Mac and Wayne Hector – was seen by Cowell as being the tune that could turn Westlife from just another boy band into a genuine force to be reckoned with, a signature song that would take them to another level. Wayne Hector told the *Hit*

Quarters website in 2010 how the song came about: 'I was out in LA doing a hip-hop session and I'd gone out for a break, and heard [*sings*] "I'm flying without wings ..." in my head, and thought, "Well, that's interesting!" So, I came up with a couple of lines for the first verse and then phoned my mama's house, left it on the answering machine and said, "Don't get rid of this!" And when I came back to England, I went into the studio with Steve and said, "Look, I've got the start of an idea. Have a listen ..." He was like, "Oh this is great!" And then he and I just sat down and said, "What is this about?" And then we said, "Well, I think this is about our wives. This is about the things that make our lives complete." And that was it. The song wrote itself. Then we finished all of the lyrics in, like, half an hour.'

There was a buzz in the industry about 'Flying Without Wings'. Several artists – including Boyzone's Stephen Gately – were known to be chasing the song. Cowell wanted it for Westlife, so he shifted into harassment mode, locking Mac and Hector in his office for two hours and hiding the key until they agreed to hand the song over to him. The song gave Westlife their third Number 1 in the space of six months and is still the track that most people associate with the group. ' "Flying Without Wings" was never a cheesy ballad,' band member Nicky Byrne said in the documentary *Westlife – Back Home*. 'It could have been a hit for anybody. Thankfully, it was ours.'

'Flying Without Wings' was voted Song of the Year for 1999 in an ITV phone-in competition; the band repaid

Mac and Hector's decision to give them the song by accidentally breaking the award across Mac's back while giving him a celebratory hug during the televised ceremony. It did indeed become the group's signature song and, what's more, it set Cowell's nostrils twitching. He felt there were sales records waiting to be broken here – and the five young Irishmen were in the perfect position to be the ones to break them.

Robson and Jerome had managed three Number 1s with their first three singles. That was a record until Irish popstrels B*Witched aced it by getting all four of their debut releases to the top of the charts. Cowell's competitive instincts kicked in – Christmas was coming and he wanted Westlife at Number 1, which would match the record, giving them a fighting chance to better it in the New Year. To give it an extra edge it would be 'The Millennium Number 1', which would mean that whoever was at the top of the charts when 1999 became the year 2000 would get maximum exposure. It would go down in history. Hedging his bets, Cowell played it safe and went for the cover-version option, in this case 'I Have a Dream', the ABBA track. Only divine intervention could stop him now.

Much to Simon's horror, that was pretty much what happened: Cliff Richard also had his eye on the Christmas/Millennium Number 1 slot and threw his hat into the ring with 'The Millennium Prayer', a song Cowell felt 'ghastly and manipulative'. Ironically, Cliff had released the song on an independent after Simon's old employers EMI refused to put it out. It duly went to

Number 1, but peaked a touch early – it was at the top of the charts some two weeks before Christmas. Cowell went all out to ensure that Richard's song didn't have a prayer of staying at the top. Simon was taking a Christmas break in Mauritius when he got the news that Westlife had won. It was, according to Cowell, the only time the music industry was pleased that he'd scored a Number 1 record.

When Westlife achieved their fifth chart topper in a row with 'Fool Again', the record was truly broken. They then proceeded to take the record out into the car park and give it a serious kicking by achieving seven Number 1s in a row.

They would have made it eight if it hadn't been for Bob the Builder. 'That was such a shock – our first Number 2. It was the first time something hadn't gone perfectly,' Shane Filan said later, recalling the day that 'What Makes a Man' was kept off the top slot. All the elements were there: it was another Wayne Hector and Steve Mac song; the video had the lads charging about in sports cars, motorbikes and helicopters; and it had the compulsory key change towards the end to give it that uplifting feeling. 'It was the first time we thought it wasn't all going to be plain sailing,' Filan recalled. 'It's a pity because – I know I'm being greedy now – the next three singles after "What Makes a Man" also went to Number 1, so, if Bob hadn't stuck his oar in, we'd have had 11 in a row.'

Denied a Number 1 record by a silly kids' TV song, Simon Cowell, given his track record, could hardly complain. He was on a roll – until Girl Thing, that is.

The group were launched by Cowell amid much hoopla

in the year 2000. They were a feisty five-piece girl band with a pop-rap sound, look and attitude that was all very reminiscent of the Spice Girls. Cowell was predicting big things for their debut single, 'Last One Standing'. He later told *Times* journalist Stephen Armstrong: 'There was always something in the pit of my stomach telling me it wasn't right, but you go along with it, hype everybody up. I spent a lot of money on the group. Everyone was expecting it to be Number 1 and it got to Number 8. A disaster. I've spent a lot of BMG's money on this and now we have a problem. I went into the office and we had a very outspoken chairman at the time, and I'm dreading the call when he's got the news. I'm just waiting to be called up. So the call comes and I hear, "All I will say to you, Simon, is this is the best thing that will ever happen in your career." And he put the phone down. It took me two hours, then I went upstairs, knocked on his door and said, "My ego is out of control, isn't it?" He said, "Yes, Simon." He could have destroyed me, he could have said, "You fucking idiot, you've blown all this money, you're not as good as you think you are." It's one of those important things you learn in your life, which is, your ego can start believing it is only you … and you don't recognise the people around you.'

Ego-wise, Simon had no great desire to be known outside of his immediate peers. He was a businessman, not a wannabe; dressing up as Wonder Dog and appearing on *Sale of the Century* had been the extent of his brushes with fame so far. That was about to change, thanks to an unlikely and unfashionable style of TV programme.

The TV talent show had experienced mixed fortunes since the glory days of the 1970s. The *grande dame* of the genre, *Opportunity Knocks*, had been on and off our screens since 1956 on both ITV and the BBC with diminishing returns. *New Faces* had ended in 1979, although a brief revival was attempted in the eighties with former winner Marti Caine as host. Singer and actor David Essex had a go at the format with his *Showcase* programme on the BBC and Jonathan Ross had even chanced his arm in 1996 with his *Big Big Talent Show*. That programme was notable for having a 'nasty' co-host in the shape of tabloid journalist Garry Bushell and the presence of future *X Factor* winner Steve Brookstein as a contestant. Granada's digital programme unit had even tried a docusoap-style show called *Rock Fillies*, following the fortunes of a manufactured girl band. None had lasted long or made any kind of deep impression on the viewing public. So there was no huge expectation for the latest incarnation: ITV's *Popstars*.

The first version of what would become the *Popstars* franchise was broadcast in New Zealand in 1999. It was a heady mix of all the best aspects of previous formats – talent finding, viewer voting and fly-on-the-wall-style real-life drama. British TV executive Nigel Lythgoe spotted the second version of the format while on holiday in Australia. He saw girl band Bardot being put together on the show and brought the idea back with him to London Weekend Television. Lythgoe – a former dancer and choreographer – was steeped in the notion of good, old-fashioned, Saturday-night, entertaining telly – something that all the family could watch. The head of press relations at LWT had a more direct, off-the-record description of the new show: 'The bastard offspring of *Big Brother* and *The Monkees.*'

Music impresario Jonathan King was originally in the running to head up the judging panel for the show – and to be the 'nasty one' in the style of Tony Hatch from *New Faces* – but he was dropped because of concerns over police investigations into his personal life. In November 2000 King was charged with sex assaults on five teenage boys. By way of coincidence, it was Simon Cowell who put up the money for King's bail – something he later said he deeply regretted.

A replacement was needed and the call then went out to none other than Simon Cowell. Nigel Lythgoe took Simon out to lunch and explained the show to him: viewers would see wannabe singers auditioned, whittled down to a shortlist, then launched as a five-piece band with all the tears and tantrums leading up to the launch of their debut single.

Cowell had experienced a taste of this kind of format the previous year, helping out with some talent-spotting for ITV's *This Morning* show after producers had decided what they needed was their own boy band. Intrigued and excited by the *Popstars* notion, Cowell said yes – as long as he got the recording rights to the finished band.

In a slight throwback to his old indecisive ways, Cowell then changed his mind. He was worried that a show like *Popstars* could expose too much of the inner workings of the industry and – strange as it seems today – he wasn't keen on appearing on screen. He got back to Lythgoe and told him he wanted out.

Cowell's cold feet left *Popstars* in the lurch. As a result, Lythgoe stepped into the role and spent the summer of 2000 on the road with pop PR Nicki Chapman and Polydor A&R man Paul Adam – who'd signed non-pop acts such as Cast and Ian Brown – auditioning would-be singers across the country for the show.

Lythgoe would later reveal that, contrary to Cowell's belief, appearing on screen was actually like taking a holiday: 'When I was running LWT entertainment, everything was about the ratings and you could never relax,' Lythgoe later revealed in an interview with *The Stage*. '*Blind Date* was a show that was doing well, but you had to keep it there. It could dip at any time and you couldn't relax about that. One of my first jobs was releasing Jeremy Beadle – that was hard. Telling someone like that who had worked for so long for the company that, I'm sorry, the company no longer wants to employ you. That has to be one of the hardest things I have done. Compared with that … appearing on shows is a breeze.'

One of the key reasons the *Popstars* format took off was the mystery surrounding who would make the cut for the final line-up of the band. That's where the 'Nasty Nigel' angle came in. 'Much better than "Nice Nigel",' Lythgoe later claimed in an interview with the *Daily Mail*. 'Much more fun to be a baddie.' In fact, Lythgoe adopted the 'Nasty' persona as a way of giving the press an angle on the show that would deflect them from identifying the five young singers who were finally chosen. *Popstars* press officer Ian Johnson later revealed the trick in a interview with the *Guardian* as the *Popstars* phenomenon began to unfold at the start of 2001: 'We need to keep the publicity pot boiling without giving too much away, and with billboards across the country proclaiming "Nigel Pick Me". What better distraction for the press than a 50-something TV executive with a cartoon on-screen identity and a bad haircut. "Nasty Nigel" is born. DJs, TV presenters and columnists all have an opinion on Nigel's audition techniques and "Nasty Nigel" is a household name.'

Simon went on his traditional December holiday. On his return to London in January he saw the capital plastered with *Popstars* posters. Then he watched the show and was immediately hooked. He saw how the series drew viewers in from the word go, with the audition process, with its occasionally deluded wannabes, to nuggets of raw talent being slowly spotted among the dross. He saw how the judges' personalities became vital to the mix – Nasty Nigel, Nurturing Nicki, Polite Paul – and how Lythgoe became the undisputed star of the show with his shocking rudeness, particularly towards contestant Kym Marsh: 'Christmas has gone, but I see the goose is still fat ...' was Nigel's comment about the singer's appearance that filled newspaper column inches for months to come. To this day, Lythgoe is still defending himself from accusations he set the 'Nasty Judge' bar too high with *Popstars*. 'I don't think it was negative,' Lythgoe told show-business writer Ben Dowell in 2010. 'Telling someone they are carrying too much weight is important if they are going to be a performer. I don't class it as belittling someone, telling them they have to lose weight. Dancers and performers nowadays are athletes. The reality of television is that you do have to be beautiful, you do have to be pretty, you do have to be attractive to the audience. It is about performance and personality.'

Marsh's shock over the remark – and the audience's – would be compounded by later revelations about the singer's issues with food: 'It's a very bad thing to do to someone,' she later told *Star* magazine. 'I'll admit I did put on weight over Christmas, but Nigel handled it very badly for someone in his position. I had an eating disorder when I was 17. I became bulimic – so I'd eat, then I'd make myself sick.' This really was reality TV – no writers required to create this drama.

As the *Popstars* series unfolded, Simon also saw the teeth-grating horror of contestant Darius Danesh mauling Britney Spears's '... Baby One More Time' and witnessed the final triumph of Marsh, Myleene Klass, Danny Foster, Suzanne Shaw and Noel Sullivan as they were moulded into the winning act – Hear'Say. Worst of all, he then saw the group's debut single 'Pure and Simple' become the fastest-selling single in UK chart history. It stayed on the charts for a whopping six months. Just one more thing to really rub it in: 'Pure and Simple' was an album track originally performed by Girl Thing. 'I still refer to the day the Hear'Say record was released as Black Monday,' Simon would later complain to the *Mirror*. 'I was so depressed. When it could have been yours, it's not a great feeling.'

Massive viewing figures, tears, triumphs and a virtually

guaranteed hit single at the end of it. Unsurprisingly, Simon Cowell was furious that he'd missed out. 'I was so mad, I thought, "I've got to do something to retaliate. I want *Popstars* off the market. I want to be on a show that's going to kick it off the air," ' Simon later confessed to *The Times*. 'That was *Pop Idol*.'

Simon didn't waste any time; his retaliation to *Popstars* would be on air by the autumn of 2001, an astonishing turnaround. First, he hooked up with a man whom he had continually promised himself he would work with: ex-Spice Girls manager Simon Fuller.

Formerly with Chrysalis records, Fuller scored his first success under his own steam with Paul Hardcastle, who's best remembered for the stuttering dance hit '19'. Further success came with singer songwriter Cathy Dennis, but Fuller would never forget that first hit and named his company 19 after the song.

The Spice Girls and Fuller had parted company in 1997, but he was doing very nicely, thank you. Unlike Cowell, Fuller had already made a huge impression on TV with his *Miami 7* show for the BBC featuring his boy/girl band S Club 7 (later called S Club). 'I started working on the idea of S Club 7 literally the day after I parted company with the Spice Girls,' Fuller later told BBC News. Fuller's brother Kim had created the series – on each episode the group sang a track from what would be their debut album. S Club 7 would go on to have seven Number 1 singles, a stunning example of harnessing the power of television to sell records.

Like Cowell, Fuller was not in the music industry to

court credibility and rave reviews. He and Cowell look alike with a shared youthful air and similar jet-black hair. Fuller is more softly spoken than Cowell, but he is just as forthright: 'My business is creating fame and celebrity,' he later told the *Guardian* in a rare interview, 'And I'm one of the best in the world. I know it to the finest detail. I reflect what's out there, and if there's a demand for something I recognise it. I don't think I'm crass. I stand by everything I do.'

Indeed, the two Simons agreed on so many things and had so much in common Cowell was concerned that, if they were to disagree over something, it wouldn't be pretty: 'A clash between two control freaks' is how Cowell predicted such a fall out would pan out. 'The problem is that we are very similar people,' he later explained to the *Mail on Sunday*. 'We both want control and success. I go through times when I don't like him much, then I see him and like him again. I've always said Fuller is the best deal-maker I've ever met. But I've always felt that I make better records.'

Although the format of *Pop Idol* would be credited to Fuller, the two Simons agreed a deal: Fuller's 19 Entertainment company would manage the winner of the show and get the TV rights, while Cowell would get the recording rights. The Simons also felt they'd improved on the format of the *Popstars* brand. 'I'd really got into *Popstars* but it was very, very clear that there was a huge weakness in the format,' Cowell said in an interview with journalist Barbara Davies. 'There wasn't an ending to the show. The real drama and tension came two-thirds of the way through when the group was selected or not selected. So I just thought, Wouldn't it be better to have a show where only one person can win? We had a better format.'

There was another upgrade he was looking for too: seeing how vital the judge's chemistry was to *Popstars*, Simon wanted to make sure *Idol* had the same, if not better. His old sparring partner Pete Waterman was an obvious choice – the pop producer's ability to pick a fight in an empty phone box would make great TV. 'I was very smart,' Cowell explained to journalist Lynda Lee-Potter. 'Because I thought, Who is the one person in the world who's got a bigger mouth than me and is fundamentally more unpleasant? Pete Waterman.'

Capital Radio DJ Neil 'Dr' Fox offered his services after hearing about the show on the media grapevine. Fox had a national profile as host of the Top 40 rundown show and, although he sometimes came across as slightly old-school and 'cheesy', he was seen as a safe pair of hands. Cowell wanted pop publicist Nicki Chapman on board – despite her association with *Popstars* – as the two had worked together at BMG. As Nigel Lythgoe was going off screen to keep his hand on the tiller as part of the 19 team, it was decided that the new panel were different enough not to be thought of as *Popstars II*.

They took the idea to ITV's controller of entertainment, Claudia Rosencrantz. A former *News of the World* writer, she'd worked her way up in television after joining as a lowly researcher and knew ITV inside out. She listened to the

Simons deliver their pitch – and said yes after hearing two minutes of it. In fact, Rosencrantz had an idea of her own to tip in: she had two presenters whose existing show wasn't working. Anthony McPartlin and Declan Donnelly had already been child actors, pop stars and kids' TV presenters but were finding the transition to grown-up TV a struggle. Their current ITV show – called *Slap Bang* – was struggling in the ratings and only six episodes were eventually made. Rosencrantz still believed in the pair but felt they'd work better as part of an ensemble rather than carrying a show on their own. 'The secret of signing talent,' she later told London's *Evening Standard*, 'is to know what you're going to do with them.' What she wanted to do with Ant and Dec was for them to present *Pop Idol*. 'We loved the idea and when we were asked we took 30 seconds to say yes,' Ant later told the *Metro* newspaper. 'We knew it would be good, but we never thought it would be as huge as it was.'

One element of the team who'd originally also said yes, then changed his mind, was Simon Cowell. He admitted his cold feet to the *Daily Mail* in 2003: 'I even made a phone call to someone at ITV at some point saying, "Would you mind if I didn't do this show?" I had seen what had happened to Nasty Nigel and I thought, he's not even nasty. I know what I'm going to be like in that situation because I haven't got that kind of patience. But they were very clear: "No, you are going to be judging this show." '

Despite some genuine last-minute interest in the show from the BBC – unsurprising, as Fuller's *Miami 7* had just been sold to America – the team stuck with ITV and the show was hurried into production. Ads were placed in the press asking for hopefuls to turn up for the first auditions in Manchester. The judging panel travelled north not really knowing if they were going to work as a team. As *Idol* was partly his baby, Cowell didn't want his position as their 'boss' to hinder their interaction: 'When we started the show,' Cowell later told *Heat* magazine, 'I just said to the other three, "The only way we are going to make this work is if we say what we feel. Don't be sycophantic. If you think I'm acting like an arsehole, say it." '

Despite this, the panel soon realised it wasn't working. It wasn't because Cowell was being an arsehole: it was, in a sense, because he wasn't. Before they got as far as the judges, the performers went through several rounds with assistant producers and producers, moving their way up the food chain to see if they were good enough or sufficiently unusual to go in front of Cowell, Waterman, Chapman and Fox. When they got that far, singers were trickling in, doing their bit and being told to wait outside while the judges deliberated; it was stiff and formal, like a Women's Institute cake competition. The singers were then called back in, given constructive feedback and given a yes or a no. Hardly the stuff of ratings-busting telly.

'We'd planned the show for months,' Simon later recalled to TV chat-show host Michael Parkinson, 'but no one had actually spoken to us as to what we were actually going to do in the audition room. So, for the first five minutes, we were quite polite. It was terrible. I said to Pete Waterman, "This is just horrendous. This is not like a real audition." '

Pete Waterman: 'When we did that first day's filming of

Pop Idol, none of us could have realised that it would ever become the biggest television show on the planet – it was a big shambles!' Waterman would later recall in the *Sun*. 'If I had not known Simon, I am sure it wouldn't have worked – because I'm the one who got Simon to be *Simon*. I called him in and said: "Sorry, Simon, if I came to you with a piece of crap, you would tell me it was a piece of crap. You've always got an opinion about everything and now, suddenly, you haven't got an opinion?" '

The judges reconvened, with Waterman's words ringing in Cowell's ears. The next contestant who appeared in front of them sang badly – and got it with both barrels. Simon had found his TV persona. 'Pete Waterman was utterly brilliant – he was better than Cowell for the first season because Simon put it on, but Waterman was *it*,' Nigel Lythgoe later revealed to the *Guardian*. 'Simon learns very quickly, though – that's his brilliance. He's a bit of a sponge.'

Television was about to find its latest Man You Love to Hate in the shape of Simon Cowell. Off screen, Nigel Lythgoe must have felt as if he were handing the crown over to Cowell. If nothing else, people would stop calling him Nasty Nigel. They never did, and, as Lythgoe told the *Mirror* in 2010: 'I don't care, to be honest. I only got that title because I was the first person to make nasty comments, back on *Popstars* in 2000. But people have been far nastier since. Do I care to name names? Absolutely … Simon Cowell.'

Bit by bit, audition by audition, the judging team were starting to develop their own personalities: 'Working on the *Pop Idol* panel with Simon Cowell, Pete Waterman and Dr Fox was like working with three naughty schoolboys,' Chapman would later recall. 'I had my hands full, that's for sure. Simon and Foxy would scribble notes to each other if a girl came on who they thought was sexy. Whereas me and Pete would write notes saying, "She's got potential", or "Bit too overbearing". We were the serious ones. But, honestly, the show was great fun to do. We laughed the whole time.'

The initial *Pop Idol* auditions would also provide another key element of the Simon Cowell image: the higher-than-average waistband. The people responsible for single-handedly creating this image were Ant and Dec. 'We didn't know Simon that well and we saw him arriving at the auditions a few times,' Dec later recounted on *This Is Your Life*. 'We kind of nudged each other and said, "Doesn't he wear his trousers enormously high?" '

FIVE
WILLIAM ROBERT YOUNG

The first series of *Pop Idol* would be defined by two auditions – one at the beginning of the process and one at the very end. They were performed by two very different young men.

When a skinny young thing with black, gel-spiked hair, barely filling his dark suit, walked into the drab audition room, Cowell recalls praying that the teenager was a good singer, since he certainly looked like the very thing they were looking for: a pop idol. Gareth Gates was a former head chorister at Bradford Cathedral; a talented multi-instrumentalist, he was young man steeped in music. He was also a young man with a devastating speech impediment. Confronted with the judges, he got as far as, 'My name's erm ...' before his stammer kicked in, leaving a huge pause – Simon Cowell was the last of the four judges to look up and see what the problem was. Cowell would later claim that the footage of Gates's audition had been heavily edited and that it actually took the 17-year-old nearly ten minutes to speak. Coaxed by Pete

Waterman, he got his name out and began to sing Westlife's signature hit 'Flying Without Wings' in a clear, sweet voice. Cowell raised his hand to bring the audition to a close: 'I'm going to stop you there. What you have done today is unbelievably brave, just standing there in front of the four of us ... you are 100 per cent coming to London for the next audition.'

Gareth Gates was a triple treat: he looked like he'd stepped off a teenage girl's wall; he could sing; and he had a back story that would develop into what would become the staple of all entertainment reality shows: 'The Journey'. In this case – brave singer overcomes terrible stammer to win the day. 'I always used to see my stammer as being a negative, all my life,' Gates later told the *Guardian*. 'But then when I went on *Pop Idol* and the first time I saw it on television, it was really, really bad. But also it made me stand out, it made people remember me. So, for the first time in my life, it worked to my advantage.'

Cowell was positive he had his *Pop Idol* right there in front of him. Later that day he phoned Simon Fuller to tell him that not only was the show going to work, but he had his next big star too.

As well as Gates there would be other memorable auditions for the team, but for rather different reasons. Young Welsh singer Rosie Ribbons would bring Pete Waterman to tears and prompt him to offer her a job on the spot after performing two songs: Maria Carey's audition staple 'Hero' and a song she'd written herself. Rik Waller would divide the panel – he may have sung like an angel but his heavyweight presence tested to the limit the idea of what a pop idol could look like. Then there was Darius Danesh, the young Scot who'd become a national laughing stock after his lack of self-control and cheesy demeanour on *Popstars*. When he exited the programme he promised he'd be back with a platinum album, yet here he was re-entering the lion's den. Clearly he was either severely misguided or in possession of levels of gumption rarely seen outside of war zones to have a crack at a place on *Pop Idol*. Simon and the panel wouldn't let him play the guitar he brought with him – typical Darius, to try to do things his way – but they voted him through anyway.

Then there were the hopefuls and the hopeless who make up the bedrock of audition shows. Caroline Buckley's chilling rendition of the Village People's 'YMCA' brought the house down; she apparently saw the audition queue and just joined it, not really knowing what it was for, but the producers were savvy enough to let her through to perform for the judges, who loved her. They didn't put her through, but she provided a much-needed injection of fun. Buckley was later hired to perform a version of the tune for a TV advert for Pizza Hut, so it was definitely worth her joining that queue. But not all of those trying out were treated with such good humour. As time grew short to get the show on air, so did Cowell's patience. His verdicts became shorter and sharper: 'The awful reality is you can't sing – that's the reality'; 'Literally, out of a hundred, I'd give that two'; 'Your outfit – and I don't mean to be rude here – is five, ten years out of date.'

He later explained to an ITV documentary celebrating 50 years of the channel why he felt justified in cutting to the chase with contestants: '*Pop Idol* is a shortcut to stardom. You can go from obscurity to household name and millionaire within three months. Along the way you've got to take a little bit of criticism. That's not a bad deal is it?'

The Caroline Buckleys of this world, who knew they had no chance, were just a bit of fun. What really intrigued Simon were the people who turned up armed with the genuine, unshakable knowledge that they had what it took to be a star. 'The fascination was just how many people had this incredible self-belief that they really were hugely talented and were going to be really famous,' Simon marvelled, 'without any talent whatsoever.'

Not all of his colleagues publicly approved of Cowell's attitude: 'I told Simon Cowell that he was too harsh,' Nicki Chapman would later tell the *Metro*. 'We all have our opinions ... that's not a bad thing, but Mr Cowell is outrageous. He is harsh but he says what he believes and it is quite a hard industry. I don't enjoy him putting people down. His comments are what he believes at the time and at least he's honest.'

Mind you, Pete Waterman was no slouch in that department, either: 'I'm not being rude,' the producer told one audition hopeful in the early stages of the competition, 'but you have the worst voice I have ever heard in my life.'

Viewing the first series of *Pop Idol* today, it's surprising how genteel it is. The audition rooms are fantastically dour and cheap-looking – the kind of places regional sales teams have their annual pep talks – and the judges' reactions to the wannabes are largely appropriate: they laugh at the funny ones, are encouraging to the talented contestants and they let down the ones that aren't cutting the mustard in a reasonable way. Cowell's comments seem pretty tame compared with the rudeness industry he has since inspired; nearly a decade later, ITV's *Dancing on Ice* judge Jason Gardiner would describe contestant Sharron Davies's performance as being like 'faecal matter that won't flush.' Now *that's* rude.

The series would also see Ant and Dec come into their own. Just as ITV executive Claudia Rosencrantz had predicted, the pair began to shine when the burden of carrying a whole show was lifted from their shoulders. Whether they were teasing the backstories out of entrants as they waited for their turns, comforting teary singers who hadn't made it through or flirting with anyone in the category of 'female and breathing', the Ant and Dec we know today were formed by their work on *Pop Idol*. Cowell's view of the pair's role in the show was that they were like 'Robin Hood – the protectors of the weak'. In turn, Ant and Dec would start to form their own impressions of Cowell: 'He's not that big a pain in the arse,' Donnelly would later reveal to music magazine *Q*. 'He's quite charming, he's got a wicked sense of humour. The biggest pain is he's always late, he keeps everybody waiting. I don't know why – he can't be doing his hair or wondering what to wear …'

On the subject of what Simon wore, Ant and Dec's observation about the height of Cowell's trousers would become a running theme throughout the series, with Donnelly dressing up as Simon for a series of sketches and sporting a pair of black trousers up to his armpits. It clearly started to rattle Cowell: 'I always wear Armani trousers and they are high-cut,' he reasoned when asked about the trouser-related teasing. 'They get stuck there a bit. I said to Ant, "Thanks, you've really given me a complex." Now I'm always looking in the mirror thinking, "Are they too high or what?" '

Auditions for the first series of *Pop Idol* concluded on 7 September 2001 in London's Docklands. The very last person to perform would provide the second of the defining auditions. Will Young was cut from remarkably similar cloth to Simon Cowell. A Home Counties prep-school boy who'd gone to Wellington College in Berkshire, Young had met Cowell before he walked into the audition room. He had entered the search for boy-band members organised by *This Morning*, as Will recalled in the diary he kept of his *Pop Idol* experience: 'Simon Cowell, a suntanned record company bigwig who I originally met on that competition on *This Morning*. He was one of the judges on that too, wonder if he recognised me? He hasn't changed much, but he's slightly more orange than last time.'

It would be astonishing if Simon didn't remember Will, as the singer had made it to the finals of the *This Morning* competition and had sung 'I'll Be There' live on the show with Cowell right in front of him.

On that final day, the producers of *Pop Idol* had told the judges that they were short of boys in the final tally and advised Simon to let through anyone they felt was borderline to even up the numbers. Unless the final guy due to sing was truly awful, he was probably going to get through. 'William Robert Young,' Pete Waterman said, in the manner of a High Court judge, 'you have come before this court today and you're the last person we're gonna see in the whole series ...'

Young then performed Michael Jackson's 'Blame It on the Boogie' in a pleasing, jazzy style while throwing some half-hearted shapes.

Nicki didn't like his dance moves (Young had been told to dance by producers the previous day). Waterman liked the version but didn't care for Will's rough-and-tumble studenty dress sense. Foxy thought he was cheesy – 'a pleasant Cheddar rather than a stinky Stilton' – and Simon declared the singer to be a good-looking boy with a nice voice. After getting a quick nod from Nigel Lythgoe, Will went through.

Further auditions were held at London's Criterion Theatre to whittle the 120 chosen performers down to 50. During this process one event occurred that showed just how much pressure the *Pop Idol* team were under to get the show on air. On 11 September, news of the terrorist attacks on the Twin Towers of the World Trade Center in New York began to trickle through – before quickly becoming a flood of information and horror. The world stood still – apart from backstage at the Criterion Theatre, where filming continued, because it was the only day they'd booked the theatre. Cowell recalls wanting to stop but Nigel Lythgoe insisted they finish the filming schedule – albeit in double-quick time.

With all this was going on, Simon had the small matter of his day job to deal with. He had become inordinately keen on a new act called Busted and saw real potential in their odd mix of bratty pop and punk. They had the songs and the style of American acts such as Blink 182, and they also delivered boy band cuteness. But, as ever, boys with guitars seemed to confuse Cowell: he couldn't get his head around the fact that the three each played guitar and that they presented themselves as a band but had no drummer. He told them to get one – they said no and went elsewhere. It later transpired there was more to the issue than merely whether they should get a drummer. 'We refused to go with Simon Cowell,' Busted's James Bourne later told journalist Johann Hari. 'We didn't want to be associated with that shit. We didn't want to be a Simon Cowell band. Then we really would have been a boy band.'

Cowell seemed genuinely disappointed that he'd lost out on Busted, predicting that they'd soon be the Number 1 pop band in Britain. They did indeed manage four Number 1s shortly afterwards, but they split three years later and are largely remembered as purveyors of novelty songs like 'Year 3000' and the theme to the movie remake of *Thunderbirds*.

Before the second – studio – phase of *Pop Idol* kicked in, Simon flew to America to see if he could generate interest in the show over there. This was an audacious move considering they didn't actually have a show yet. 'We pitched it as the American Dream,' he later told the US current affairs show *60 Minutes*. 'The person who's likely to win will be a cocktail waitress, can't get a deal, talented

... and within 20 weeks will become the most famous person in this country. It was a very good pitch, I thought, but not good enough because everyone threw us out of their offices.'

Seemingly it hadn't occurred to Simon that anyone would turn him down. Given that all he actually had was a series of audition tapes of middling to bad singers, in retrospect it's hardly surprising the US networks didn't bite his hand off. Cowell was winded by the experience; Simon Fuller, on the other hand, felt they were in the right and that the Americans would eventually come round to their way of thinking.

Cowell returned to Britain just as the first episode of *Pop Idol* was about to go on air. ITV organised a showing of the opening programme for journalists, to create a buzz before the first transmission. It was a hit. The mix of the judges was right, there was a good balance of genuine talent and no-hopers and the presence and humour of Ant and Dec prevented the dry, documentary feel that slightly spoiled the fun of *Popstars*.

At the start of the *Pop Idol* process, Simon Cowell was the support act. All the other judges had public profiles, while Cowell's was virtually nonexistent. Given the previous experience of Nigel Lythgoe, it was highly likely that this would change dramatically once *Pop Idol* went on air. No one remembers Paul Adam, one of the judges on the *Popstars* panel – but everyone remembers Nasty Nigel.

Simon figured he needed some advice – and maybe even some protection – in relation to dealing with the media. The man who could advise the likes of Westlife on how to put themselves across – down to the tiniest detail – had no idea how to put himself across to the media. He was also concerned his newfound fame would bring skeletons out of his closet. He turned to PR guru Max Clifford for help.

Clifford was a local-newspaper sports reporter before turning his hand to publicity and PR, establishing his own agency in 1970. He claims he has never had to pitch for business since then. His stock in trade is the lurid tabloid front-page splash – whether it be claims over footballer David Beckham's private life or former government minister David Mellor having sex while wearing a Chelsea football kit. The old-chestnut headline of FREDDIE STARR ATE MY HAMSTER from the *Sun* in 1986 is still proudly displayed on his company website. For a man who boasts of how well respected he is in media, his opinion of the press was and is spectacularly low: 'We have the most vicious press in the world,' he later made clear in the *Radio Times*. 'Journalists, particularly on tabloids, are miserable, frightened for their jobs, alcoholics etc. At press awards they jeer, boo, fight and get pissed – and that's the cream. Nice ones no longer succeed. Everyone stabs each other. Journalism is bloody horrible. The unions are destroyed, so individuals have no power. They do what they're told or they're out. You've got a lower quality of human being who'll do anything for a story. It's sad.'

Given that Simon Cowell was about to become very famous indeed – and that ITV has a very effective PR operation of its own – he hardly needed Clifford to promote him or his career. Cowell says he went to Clifford because he was worried about stories from his past being sold to the tabloids. 'You've got to remember, I started sleeping with girls when I was 17,' Cowell explained to *Heat* magazine when his fame kicked in. 'In the 25 years since then I have had a number of girlfriends. Most of them are very nice and wouldn't go to the newspapers. The ones you see in the papers are mostly one-night stands. In my career I want to be successful and *Pop Idol* is a way of enabling my career to become more successful. You're obviously going to get that much more publicity being on the show, so I can't criticise anyone who has written a story about an ex-girlfriend. I can, however, criticise some of the girls, because there are one or two who have said things which are just lies.'

When former Page Three girl Georgina Law's story of her liaison with Cowell appeared in the *Sunday Mirror* soon afterwards, it looked like a classic kiss-and-tell. In fact, she did the story with Cowell's OK. 'I met Simon at the Spearmint Rhino club, where I used to work occasionally as a lap dancer. This was before *Pop Idol*, so he wasn't famous, and I certainly didn't get together with him because of his name. He is a lovely man – very charming and funny – and we had a casual relationship for about six months. We weren't proper boyfriend and girlfriend, but we'd see each other regularly. Simon was great, he'd take me out for dinner and buy me presents – we even had a wonderful weekend in Paris. But after about six months, we agreed to split up but remain friends. Then

Pop Idol came out, and suddenly there were lots of stories about Simon in the papers. A lot of them mentioned me, and contained quotes from me that I'd never said. Some other stories said really nasty things about Simon too – one girl did a story saying he was terrible in bed, which isn't true. I hated that – so I decided to sell my story to set the record straight.'

Stories like these of course represent a double whammy for Max Clifford: he also represents Spearmint Rhino. But Clifford is about protection as well as promotion: 'I censor things as well,' he would later explain about his work. 'For every story I break, I stop a dozen – sometimes because those involved are paying me a fortune, or I don't think they deserve to be destroyed, or I know it's untrue. I'm good at covering up anything I don't want people to know. The biggest part of my work is damage limitation.'

Not all the stories about Simon's sex life benefited from a positive PR spin. Glamour model Debbie Corrigan – a former girlfriend of comic Jim Davidson no less – slated Simon in a kiss-and-tell classic in the *People*. In a tabloid headline that was just waiting to happen, she branded Cowell a FLOP IDOL in bed. 'Making love to Simon is like going on a cross-Channel ferry,' she said. 'He rolls on. He rolls off. And frankly I felt sick throughout. Simon seems to think he is some sort of sex god. Personally I think he's the spitting image of Dale Winton. In words that Simon would understand, he's not good enough. He's not a bedroom idol; I wouldn't even give him one. Now I laugh when I see him telling people

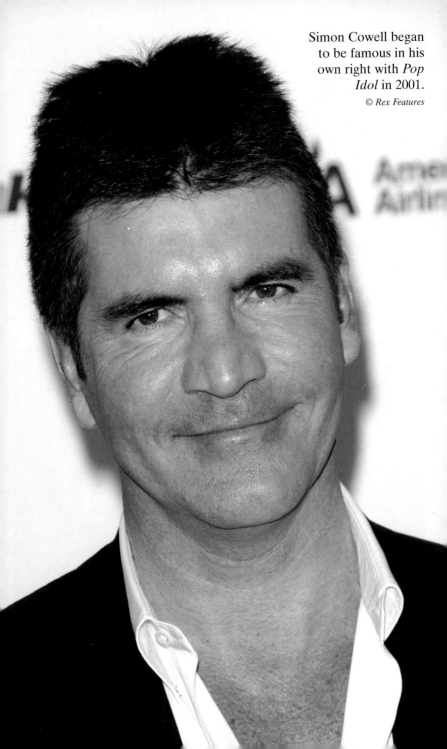

Simon Cowell began to be famous in his own right with *Pop Idol* in 2001.

© *Rex Features*

Above: Cowell's fellow judges included Pete Waterman, who he'd known back in the 1980s. ©*Rex Features*

Below: A family in the spotlight – Cowell with mother Julie and brother Nicholas in 2007. © *Rex Features*

Above: Early success for Cowell included promoting Sinitta. © *Rex Features*

Inset: Sinitta at her '80s best. © *Rex Features*

Jackie St Clair would
become another key
friend for Cowell.

© Rex Features

Above: Cowell signed IOYOU – here in their-better known phase as Westlife.
© Rex Features

Below: Having missed out on the Spice Girls, Cowell tried to make up for it by putting together 5ive. From left to right, Breen, Richard Neville, Scott Robinson, Sean Conlon and Jason Brown.
© Rex Features

Above: Will Young – the first ever *Pop Idol*. © *Rex Features*

Below: Friend, colleague and fellow mogul Louis Walsh with, left, Ronan Keating. © *Rex Features*

Above: Walsh and Cowell away from their *X Factor* duties. © *Rex Features*

Below: One sure sign that Cowell had made it was his guest appearances in *The Simpsons*.

© *Rex Features*

Cowell with ex-girlfriend Terri Seymour.

on *Pop Idol* they're rubbish. I just sit there thinking his own performance isn't that hot either. Sorry, Simon, but you just haven't got it. That was, as you might say, one of the worst performances I've ever had.'

Back at *Pop Idol* a little damage limitation would be required to keep the show's format on track. The first episode was broadcast on Saturday, 6 October, and the mix of judges was going down a storm. Unbelievably, it was then decided to jettison the judging element of the show after the initial audition stage. The idea would be for Simon and the others to just pop up and offer a few words of encouragement to the hopefuls. All the zing and tension provided by the judges and contestants clashing would be sucked out of the show, essentially leaving it as a mere music showcase. Cowell felt the idea was stupid and was shocked that this hadn't been thought through at such a late stage. As the final 50 were put through their paces, sharper-eyed viewers noticed that Simon and the other judges suddenly took a back seat. They weren't the only ones: ITV's Claudia Rosencrantz noticed too and she was not best pleased. One phone call later and the judges were back at the centre of the programme. The day-to-day producers may not have understood who was at the heart of the programme, but she did. Rosencrantz put her finger firmly on the show's appeal when telling the London *Evening Standard* about her six-year-old daughter: 'She plays *Pop Idol* every night – she is Simon Cowell and her toys all have to perform.'

If the judges hadn't been around for the middle stages of

the competition – where the 50 were hacked down to the final ten – then a pivotal moment in the show would never have happened. Simon was by now totally convinced that Gareth Gates would win, to the extent of letting other talent pass him by. When Will Young stepped in front of the judges to sing his sparkling, jazzy take on The Doors' 'Light My Fire', all of the panel liked it except Cowell. 'Distinctly average' was Cowell's opinion of Young's performance. 'I had a vision of Sunday lunch and after Sunday lunch you saying to your family, "I'm now going to sing a song for you." In the context of this show I honestly didn't think it was good enough.'

A baffled Young – who'd already discussed with his family what he'd do if Simon was rude to him – was encouraged by judge Nicki Chapman to answer back. So Young did just that: 'I love disagreeing with Simon, 'cos I do it every week, but all of us have been dying to say things to you,' he said, gearing up to say his piece.

Cowell then started to justify his comments but was sharply cut off by Will: 'Sorry, can I finish? Thank you. I think it's nice that you've given opinions in this show – I think in previous shows you haven't, you've given projected insults and it's been terrible to watch. I think in this show you've been better and I think you have given opinions and I think you've backed up your opinions – which is what the other three do, which is what I respect. It is your opinion but I don't agree with it – I don't think it was average. I don't think you could ever call that average. But it is your opinion and I respect that, so thank you very much.'

The two Home Counties kids had clashed – very politely, mind – and Will Young had come out on top. Even Cowell had to admit that Young had got the better of him: 'You are a gentleman, sir,' he said as the singer exited to a hero's welcome in the greenroom. Young, who had so far lurked in the shadows of the show, was instantly transformed into its leading light – the singer who dared to stand up to Simon Cowell. 'I would have always been my own person,' Young later told the *Digital Spy* website. 'I think people could tell that from the time on *Pop Idol* when I had a bit of a scuffle with Simon Cowell. They saw that I was up for a bit of a fight. I think British people like honesty and I think people still like the fact that I stood my ground on *Pop Idol*.'

When Cowell watched the confrontation back on TV, he realised he'd seriously misjudged the situation. Young sounded great and had made him look foolish – Simon had been so convinced that Gates was the winner, he'd lost sight of a great talent that was right there in front of him. 'I've never, ever resented anyone having a go back at me,' Cowell later stated in an interview with *Heat* magazine. 'I think, "At least you've got the guts to say it to my face." '

Will sailed into the final list of 10 *Pop Idol* performers, joining Aaron Bailey, Rosie Ribbons, Rik Waller, Zoe Birkett, Laura Doherty, Jessica Garlick, Hayley Evetts, Gareth Gates and Chris Niblett, who performed under the name of Korben. They were heading for the final stages of the series, the live knockout shows that started in the run up to Christmas 2001. What unfolded over these final weeks was a drama of epic proportions. Korben was the first to go; the flamboyant singer's take on George Michael's 'A Different Corner' was judged to be not up to scratch by both the public and the judges. Korben himself thought otherwise – newspapers had outed him as gay on the run-up to the show. 'I didn't declare my sexuality – it was only after it had been publicly outed that everybody knew,' he told the BBC straight after the show. 'I think without that there would have been a pretty good chance of my getting through. It's a shame that people are steered towards that way of thinking, but I think times are changing – just not quickly enough for me.'

The following week's Christmas show saw the surprise return – yet again – of Darius Danesh after the heavyweight Rik Waller had to pull out because of throat problems. Cowell had a real soft spot for the smooth young Scotsman and knew that his return would make 'great telly'. Jessica Garlick – whom Cowell believed to be 'a bit safe' – was the next casualty. The cull continued into the New Year, as, one by one, the young singers were dropped. Each would briefly become the most famous person in Britain until the next to leave was announced and the focus shifted to them.

On the big band show on 19 January, Gareth Gates sang 'Mack the Knife', Simon's favourite song of all time; it was clear whom Cowell wanted to become the eventual Pop Idol. Darius's charmed run finally came to an end on 2 February; he left with a flourish, as ever, promising to return even bigger and better.

In a publicity coup, Young and Gates were sent on the

road in the style of campaigning politicians, asking for the public's votes on the final days of the series. It was the best pop story the nation's press had seen since Blur versus Oasis in 1995. In fact, in the loftier pages of the broadsheet press, the *Pop Idol* final was played out along very similar lines as the great Britpop battle of the nineties: posh, privileged Will versus working class 'real' Gareth.

The 26-week *Pop Idol* experience finally came to an end on Saturday, 9 February 2002. Simon had commissioned Swedish songwriter Jörgen Elofsson to suggest a tune that would sum up how the singers would feel at the very moment they were performing on the live final. It would in turn be released as a single straight after the programme, sung by the winning artist. Elofsson – a trusted pair of hands after penning hits for Britney Spears, Geri Halliwell and Steps – suggested 'Evergreen', a song originally written for Westlife, with its chorus celebrating seizing the moment. Cowell loved it. When he played it to Will Young, Cowell claims the singer didn't care for the song, branding it a 'pop record'.

Despite this, both Gareth and Will sang 'Evergreen' on the final show; all that the two young singers could do after they'd performed was to wait for the viewers' verdict. Simon Cowell had the last word on the whole emotional experience: 'Two winners, the most amazing production team, the best five months of my life and I want to thank ITV because without them this show wouldn't be on TV.' He couldn't resist one last dig, though: 'I still think that Pete Waterman is talking a load of old you know what!'

The final, lasting image of the series would be Will Young's face – wide-eyed shock plastered across it and mouth agape – as it was announced that he had won. Against the odds, he was the Pop Idol. 'I just wanted to burst into tears,' he later wrote in his book *Anything Is Possible*. 'I clapped my hands to my face and stared around in disbelief. Everything happened in slow motion. I turned to Gareth and hugged him, then Ant and Dec. I could see my family were going mental in the audience.'

As judge Neil Fox later told *Digital Spy*, the first series of *Pop Idol* is still looked upon very fondly by both the public and those who took part. It had a charm and a straightforward appeal that appears to have been lost over the years as the format became fine-tuned. There was something very pure about *Pop Idol*,' Fox said. 'I think there was a simplicity there – programmes like *X Factor* have become very successful, but there are a lot of gimmicks in these other shows, and I think there was something very pure about *Pop Idol*. It was very simple, public vote, no games, you couldn't fix it by the judges saying "save this person, save that person". It was very pure: public didn't like the person, out they go. Luckily in the first series we ended up with two very good people in the final.'

Simon and the team at 19 had the option to sign anyone in the final ten – unsurprisingly they snapped up Gareth Gates backstage, moments after he'd heard the news he had lost the competition to Will. 'When Will won, Gareth was in pieces and there were a lot of tears,' Cowell recalled in an interview with *The Daily Mail* two years later. 'Then

I went to see Will and it was awkward because he knew I'd wanted Gareth to win. I was gutted when Gareth lost. I let my emotions take over my business brain and with hindsight I was the one to blame, not Will. He knew that I was going to sign the winner but I was so outwardly supporting Gareth. There was always a distance between me and Will.'

Darius Danesh was also offered a deal; he turned it down because he felt he was being pushed down the route of being a cover version singer. 'I probably got on best with Darius out of all the contestants we have ever had,' Simon later told the *Mirror*. 'The only thing I disagreed with was his musical direction, where I advised him not to write his own material; it was friendly advice.'

'I don't hate Simon Cowell,' Darius told the *Guardian* shortly after the dust had settled from the series. 'Sometimes what you see on television isn't exactly what the person is like in real life, so although you've seen him be nasty on TV to some of the contestants, in real life he's a gentleman with manners. He's just brutally honest and quite cruel for the effect of entertaining, I suppose.'

Three weeks after the final – they didn't turn things around quite as quickly in those days – 'Evergreen' went to Number 1. It had sold more than 1.1 million copies – a new record – and it stayed in the charts for 16 weeks. What's more, Simon Cowell had become the most famous man in Britain. He was about to become one of the most famous people in the world. One US network had come back and said yes to the American version of the show: 'We've been talking to Fox in America,' Cowell confirmed, 'and they said, "I think you should be chairman of the panel in America." If that helps make the show more interesting, I will do it.'

SIX

OLD MR HIGH TROUSERS HIMSELF

Television folklore has it that it was the daughter of media mogul Rupert Murdoch who persuaded him to bring the *Pop Idol* format to America's Fox network after ABC, CBS and NBC had passed on the show. Murdoch is the global media owner of News Corporation, which includes BSkyB, 20th Century Fox and News International titles such as the *Sun*, the *News of the World* and *The Times*. Daughter Elisabeth, a TV executive in her own right, is credited with bringing the show to her dad's attention.

Fox's head of reality shows, Mike Darnell, has since said that version is a myth and that the network had already decided to take the show after an impressive pitch by Simon Fuller. *Pop Idol* was, in Darnell's view, a major improvement on other shows already on US television. Warner Brothers had aired an American version of *Popstars* in 2001 that had seen the creation of an all-girl band called Eden's Crush – future Pussycat Doll Nicole Scherzinger was a member. ABC and MTV also had a go at the format with their *Making the Band* show, which started in 2000 and ran for most of the decade. The first act created was O-Town, who managed four Top 40 hits in the UK. 'I liked both of them [*Popstars* and *Making the Band*] for two or three weeks,' Darnell told a BAFTA audience in London in 2007. 'But, when the auditions were over, they became very girly, with all the contestants living together,' Darnell said. 'What Simon was pitching was one big long audition, and I liked that.'

Elisabeth Murdoch has since confirmed that the reality is slightly different from the legend: 'I don't understand how it's gotten slightly so out of control,' she told the *New York Times* in 2008. 'Because all I was doing was watching TV enthusiastically. I happened to call my dad in the middle [of *Pop Idol*] because I was so excited. And he said, "Oh, I think someone's shown that to us." I said, "You have got to buy it." As one does when you chat with your family, you are very direct. So I was very direct. So Dad went off and said, "You have to buy this show." And therein lies the luck of television.'

It was then Fox's bad luck that, after it had agreed to take the show, its chief asset then changed his mind – yet again – and didn't want to appear on screen. Just as he had with *Popstars*, Simon Cowell initially agreed to do the American version of *Idol*, but then almost immediately had second thoughts: 'First of all, I said yes,' he later recalled to CNN's Larry King. 'And then I thought, Oh, I don't want to go through this again – I've done it once in England. Let somebody else do it.'

Given the amount of work Simon Fuller had put into

securing the deal, Cowell was sweet-talked into going along with the show. When he got to America and saw the set-up, Cowell's first thought was to change his mind once more. The view of the US producers was: if the British version had been a success, then they should copy it down to the last detail. There were four judges on *Pop Idol*, so *American Idol* had to have four as well. When Cowell arrived two were already in place: pop star and choreographer Paula Abdul and musician and talent scout Randy Jackson.

Between 1988 and 1991 Abdul racked up six US Number 1s with her harmless R'n'B pop. She had fared less well in the UK and was best known for the Grammy-winning 'Opposites Attract' video, in which she danced with a cartoon cat. She had also been involved in a legal battle from a backing singer who claimed that that she had sung 'co-lead' vocals on Abdul's debut album, though Abdul had won the case.

It would take time for Cowell to warm to Abdul, but he knew straightaway that he and Jackson were on the same wavelength. 'Randy is incredibly important on the panel because he has, to use an American expression, great energy,' was Cowell's assessment of Jackson when asked by the *New York Times*. 'And it's very easy to be cynical and down and depressed when you're on this show, and I've never ever seen Randy down.'

Jackson had a staggering CV and had worked with everyone from Bruce Springsteen to Mariah Carey, something he liked to mention. A lot. 'I'd heard about him [Cowell] because I'd done A&R for a long time over in the UK,' Jackson later told ITV's Trevor McDonald. 'I realised

I actually really liked this guy. He was smart and savvy about music.'

The American producers were so keen to replicate the four-judge format that they didn't seem to be too concerned about who made up the numbers. Cowell later recalled that there were several deeply unsuitable candidates trying out for the role. One was an ultra-serious New York rock writer who, within minutes of meeting, Simon knew was totally unsuitable for the pop-centred format. Another was a musician and performer whose chief skill was that he could do impressions of cartoon characters. Appalled by just how wrong the candidates were, he begged Nigel Lythgoe – who'd gone over to the US as part of the deal – to stick to three judges.

The other issue were the hosts. Given that there were two hosts on *Pop Idol* – and they were funny – so *American Idol* had to have the same number and guaranteed laughs had to be part of the package. The two presenters in place were Ryan Seacrest and Brian Dunkleman. Seacrest – an experienced DJ and TV presenter – had the blonde locks and chiselled cheekbones of a boy band singer and an unremitting air of enthusiasm. However, that enthusiasm didn't stretch as far as Cowell himself – Seacrest would later tell the E! channel that his first impressions of Simon were not that good: 'I looked at this guy and he was full of himself and his pants were up to his bellybutton and he's smoking cigarettes and I thought, "Who is this character? There's no way he's going to work over here in the States." '

To Simon, Dunkleman – a dark-haired actor and stand-up

comedian – seemed out of place, and he noticed that the two presenters lacked the chemistry displayed by Ant and Dec. There was a straightforward reason for this: Seacrest and Dunkleman had met only the day before. 'I guess some executive at Fox who I pitched to remembered me and wanted me to come in and audition for *Idol*,' Dunkleman later told AOL TV. 'So I had no idea what the show was. I came in late in the process and I auditioned and I tested, and literally the next day I was on set. There was a lot of comedians, but it was also a lot of people who had broadcast experience. Ryan came in late in the process, too. I actually met him the day after I tested, and then we went in and we tested together, and the next day we were working.'

Cowell was shocked. Ant and Dec had worked together since then were child actors; their onscreen chemistry was one of the key factors of the *Pop Idol* success story. The American equivalent was to chuck a DJ and a comic together and hope for the best.

Auditions were lined up for Los Angeles, New York, Atlanta, Dallas, Seattle, Chicago and Miami. Once the auditions got under way another problem arose: the fixed-grin, American politeness of his fellow judges.

The very first person to walk into an *American Idol* audition was given the soft-soap treatment – even if Abdul and Jackson didn't totally care for the song or the performance, they *rillly, rilly liked* the performer himself. Cowell was appalled and reverted to his factory setting of direct and to the point. In a clipped, slightly more upmarket voice than he used on British television, Cowell gave it to the young singer straight: 'I think that we have to tell the truth here, which is that this singer is just awful. Not only do you look terrible but you sound terrible. You're never going to be a pop star in a million years.'

Simon would later describe the silence in the room after he had given that first verdict as eerie; Paula Abdul in particular was appalled at Cowell's attitude towards the contestant. Simon claims she actually offered the rather brilliant reason that he couldn't speak to contestants like that because, 'This is America.'

Simon's demeanour seemed to genuinely upset his hosts and his attitude seemed to fascinate them in equal measure; but he knew exactly what his role was within the show's format, as he later explained to US television journalist Anderson Cooper: 'Ninety-nine per cent of people who watch the show are in the same position as me – they know when something is good or not. I rely on my instincts.'

During the first series of *Idol*, the auditions were relatively laid-back, low-key affairs, very much like *Pop Idol*. That was to change radically after one incident: 'There were three or four guys who had been slated by me in New York who got together outside the audition rooms with baseball bats,' he later told *OK!* magazine. 'I had no idea about this until the following day, when one of the production crew said: "You were lucky last night!" '

There were even more serious reports of an armed man in the vicinity of the auditions too, but these were played down by Cowell. 'The death threat thing came because someone had got into the studios where we record *American Idol* and he was brandishing a gun. Someone said as a joke, "I think they're here for Simon!" and it just kind of escalated.' As a result of incidents like these, hefty security was introduced during the first series. It's been there ever since.

As the auditions progressed and Cowell continued in the same vein he had perfected in Britain – but a bit posher and a touch ruder – the mood began to darken and there were fears among Nigel Lythgoe and the production team that Paula Abdul was about to walk out. In fact Cowell became so exasperated by Abdul's 'patronising' of the contestants, it was he who was the first to walk off set. The tears and tensions between Cowell and Abdul continued as they flew between the host cities. Randy Jackson told *Entertainment Tonight* by way of explanation, 'Part of it's his personality, part of it's his English humour. You can say to someone in England, "Oh my God, you're fat, get off the TV," and people will die laughing. Over here, people will be like, "You know what? That wasn't really a nice thing to say." '

Eventually a confrontation ended with Abdul crying in her dressing room. A summit was later called between the judges and Nigel Lythgoe. Cowell put his case that they were there as on-air A&R advisers and it was their job to tell the truth for the sake of the audience and the contestants, whether that meant being honest to the point of brutality or championing a singer they genuinely believed in. The mood settled, filming began to run more smoothly and Abdul got on board with the show's concept. 'It's easy to be an asshole on TV,' Cowell later explained in an interview back home in *The Times*. 'But, after a while, people could see I wasn't trying to be rude. I was actually truthful in what I was saying. As long as you're saying what people are thinking, you're no longer an idiot.'

Not everyone agreed: co-host Brian Dunkleman would later express concerns over the way contestants on the show were treated. 'That doesn't just fall on Simon,' he said. 'I think the whole concept of that first season was these kids had no idea what the show was. They just knew that somebody was going to get a recording contract. But basically what the producers were doing was, they were pre-screening every kid, and then they would take the people who were actually talented. But they were *really* looking for the people that weren't, that were just awful. So, to me, they were just setting them up, making them think they were good enough and then putting them in front of the judges.'

One person who was definitely good enough to be put in front of the judges was 20-year-old Kelly Clarkson. By the time the circus had reached Houston, judges seemed to have settled into the roles and accepted each other's quirks: Simon was rude, Paula was potty, Randy Jackson was a confirmed name dropper. When Clarkson walked in and told the panel she was going to sing 'Express Yourself', the seasoned session bass player couldn't help himself: 'I worked on that song with Madonna,' he said, causing Abdul and Cowell to crack up. With just the right combination of charm and sass, Clarkson belts out her *a cappella* version of the song. To show how much relations had improved among the judges by that stage, the audition then degenerated into a knockabout piece of business, with Clarkson replacing Jackson at the judges' table and giving her verdict on his singing abilities. All three eventually put Clarkson through; Cowell can't resist a bit of rudeness though: 'Yes to Hollywood on one condition,' he told her.

'As long as you tell Ryan [Seacrest] out there that he needs to redo his highlights.'

This Clarkson duly did ('Score!' she cried) and the judges made a note of a genuine prospect – not really a winner, just a good strong contender – not only because of her voice but also because of her attitude. Bar worker Clarkson, literally, was the cocktail waitress with talent that Cowell had envisaged in his 'American Dream' pitch to Fox. Other members of the *Idol* team noticed her too: 'She has an outstanding voice, and she has a personality,' Simon Fuller later commented to the *Guardian*, adding the waspish punchline, 'Relative to most Americans …'

Back in Britain, viewers hungry for a fix of music reality were delighted to hear that they there were about to get a fresh dose – but Simon Cowell wasn't going to be involved. The second instalment of *Popstars* was about to get under way, this time styled as *The Rivals*. After failing to secure DJ Chris Evans and rock manager and reality-show star Sharon Osbourne as judges, the producers settled on the slightly rum combination of Pete Waterman, Westlife manager Louis Walsh and ex-Spice Girl Geri Halliwell. Davina McCall from *Big Brother* was on board as presenter. Simon believed strongly that the problem with the first series of *Popstars* was that there were too many singers to focus on – that's why his series had only one Pop Idol. The new *Popstars* show looked set to compound this problem, by putting together two groups. Simon also wasn't too keen on the mix of judges: 'I had one of the tapes sent over to America because I love Louis and Pete and they're really good friends of mine,' he admitted to

*OK! m*agazine. 'I couldn't believe my eyes. Pete was in floods of tears, Louis was crying, Davina was crying and Geri Halliwell was just talking a load of rubbish. I like the show but I was just amazed.'

Things were running much more smoothly on the other side of the Atlantic. As the American series of *Idol* began to go on air, viewers and the US media very quickly became fascinated by Simon Cowell.

'*American Idol* is a huge hit with the ratings sky-rocketing week after week,' *E! News* presenter Giuliana Rancic told viewers as *Idol* fever kicked in. 'Simon Cowell's judging style can be harsh, but ironically it's made him more popular than some contestants.'

American Idol co-host Ryan Seacrest later told CNN, 'He's popular because he does something that most people are afraid to do. And that is say what's on his mind. I think his honesty, his candour is something that people like to hear.'

The Cowell candour was making him the undoubted star of the show. Paula Abdul hired a scriptwriter to pen her some one-liners to try to keep up with Simon's jibes – unsurprisingly, they fell flat. One referred to Simon being affected by 'Mad Cowell's Disease' – and that was one of the better ones.

Trying to help, the production team even presented Simon with an unsolicited script filled with pithy put-downs for him to use, assuming that his critiques were rehearsed before hand. He sent them away, making it clear that their scripted insults would not be required. 'I think the great thing about this show is that words are not put in our mouths,' he told a press conference as the show reached the final stages. 'I think Fox has been incredibly brave in that respect. They're allowing us to do what we do in real life – argue, agree sometimes, try to create some stars. But I'm telling you now, whoever wins this competition – and you can remember these words – I think will have one of the fastest-selling records of all time. I really do believe that. I think the important thing at the moment is just to get past this series – make this one work. Because these competitions work if we really, really create a star at the end. Otherwise, there's no credibility to the show. It's all a complete waste of time.'

Cowell's prediction was about to be put to the test as the final ten contestants were put through their paces. Despite his bullish attitude when he was speaking to the press, he was distinctly underwhelmed by the quality of the finalists. 'I think you looked ordinary out there,' he told contestant Jim Verraros. 'I think if you were to win this competition then we have failed.' Cowell was bang on the money, as Verraros went out on the first week of the finals. Simon saw only two real contenders: Justin Guarini – a killer package of corkscrew curls and winning charm – and the stunning diva Tamyra Gray. To the astonishment of Cowell, the contestants and a large slice of the viewing public, Gray went out of the competition in fourth place. Seemingly from nowhere, Kelly Clarkson had cut through the competition to face Guarini in the final showdown.

In September 2002, some 23 million people watched the final of *American Idol*. Stretched over two nights from the Kodak Theatre in Hollywood – where the Oscars are held – the glitz and glamour were set to stun and the show made the British version look pretty tame in comparison. What the show didn't have though was the genuine drama of *Pop Idol*. Though Will Young and Gareth Gates were seen as evenly matched, it was a genuine shock when Young won. *American Idol* was a virtual walk in the park for Kelly Clarkson as she outperformed Justin Guarini at every level. Simon had to admit that, although she was a worthy winner, Clarkson had surprised him and he admitted as much to reporters after the show: 'Hopefully, we've got one person – that's all that matters, one person – who really is a genuine star at the end of this competition. I think we probably have. But, no matter what anyone tells you, the fact was that this girl was not on the radar until she made the Top 10.'

Part of the Simon's original pitch was that the show would definitely result in a massive hit single for the winning act. Cowell hedged his bets with Kelly Clarkson and made her debut a double-A-sided single: 'Before Your Love', co-written by UK singer and songwriter Cathy Dennis, and 'A Moment Like This', co-written by Cowell stalwart Jörgen Elofsson, who penned Will Young's 'Evergreen'. Once again, the Swedish songwriter seemed to sum up the mood of the competition and his song became the lead track. The proof that Simon was right came when the single performed the biggest leap in *Billboard* chart history since The Beatles' 'Can't Buy Me Love' in 1964 – another record broken for Cowell. The success of the single vindicated all of the claims that the Simons had predicted when they pitched the show – they had cracked the American market in one move. Game, set and match to Simon Cowell.

It seemed he could do no wrong – so enthralled were

Americans with the Cowell critique, one man even offered Simon money to judge his most intimate of performances. 'I was once offered money to judge someone in bed – a couple,' he later told Fox News. 'I stupidly turned it down, about a hundred grand – I should have taken the money.'

The US media – by now also having taken Simon to their collective bosoms – were desperate to know if he would be back for a second series. 'I'm definitely interested,' he said. 'The problem is that I also work for a company back in England. And they have to approve of this. But I don't think there will be a problem.'

There wasn't a problem, other than the fact that Fox wanted a second series on air in five months' time, a punishing turnaround by anyone's standards. Six weeks after the *American Idol* final, filming started on Series Two, this time without co-host Brian Dunkleman. There was enough buzz about the first series to keep the American public occupied. As well as Clarkson's single, there was a US tour featuring the final artists, a TV special and a movie, *From Justin to Kelly*, starring the two *Idol* finalists. This was one case where the team stretched things a little too thinly. The film, written by Simon Fuller's brother Kim (who wrote the film *Spice World*), was a glorified beach movie and performed badly at the box office. Clarkson was clear about her reasons for doing the film: 'Two words – contractually obligated!' she told *Time* magazine. 'I knew when I read the script it was going to be real, real bad, but when I won I signed that piece of paper, and I could not get out of it.'

Cowell's American odyssey would have one far longer-term success than Justin's and Kelly's film careers: his relationship with Terri Seymour, a willowy, husky-voiced brunette with that exotic look that Cowell always seems drawn to. Seymour, raised by her single mum Margaret in Little Chalfont in Buckinghamshire, had been a model from the age of 12 and had done catwalk work for designer Vivienne Westwood while she was still at school. She'd also appeared in pop videos for George Michael and Soul II Soul, had been a hostess on TV game show *Wheel of Fortune* and had played herself in the movie *24 Hour Party People*. Since then she'd moved to the States and picked up work as a television presenter and model; she was shooting a commercial when she came across Cowell. It wasn't the first time they'd met: Seymour first encountered Cowell when she was 18. 'He was actually dating my best friend back then,' Terri later told the *Daily Mail*. 'They only went out a couple of times, but the very first time I met him, I thought he was the funniest person I'd ever met. Whenever we saw each other it was always as part of a massive group of friends, and, to be honest, I hadn't really fancied him before. We lost touch over the years, but bumped into each other again later and, when I had to come to LA to do a commercial, Simon and I met up for dinner and he said that I could stay with him if I wanted. We spent more and more time together and then, one day, there was just this moment that it happened. We'd sit outside the house every night and have drinks and this one day, I thought to myself, "Oh, I really like him." Luckily, he felt the same way and that, really, was that.'

When the pair began to be photographed together by the paparazzi, Seymour found herself in demand as an interviewee as well as an interviewer. One question was on everyone's mind: 'What is it like to date Simon Cowell?' Terri said on US TV show *Live and Direct*, 'I would say, interesting, hard work. I like to think I keep him grounded, or at least I try. He's always very honest and can say things maybe in a way that we wouldn't say them; he can be a little harsh sometimes. He says things the wrong way. He's always critiquing me; I give him as good as he gets. He's not good at taking it, though; he can dish it out but he's not so good at taking it.'

As the second series of *American Idol* was gearing up, the live finals of *Popstars: The Rivals* were going out on ITV in the UK. The producers of the second series had come up with a neat idea – the climax of the programme would be a battle between the two created groups for the hallowed Christmas Number 1 slot in the UK charts. Another nice touch was that each act would be mentored by one of the judges. The hopefuls had been whittled down to two groups – a boy band called One True Voice, who were being looked after by Pete Waterman, and a group of girls, whose mentor was Louis Walsh, given the name Girls Aloud. One of the singers chosen for the girl band – Cheryl Tweedy, a council-estate kid from Newcastle – recalled how she felt the day the band members were finally put in place: 'The only word I can use to describe the feeling was euphoric,' Tweedy said in the band autobiography *Dreams That Glitter*. 'It was amazing, almost like a buzz going through my body. I couldn't believe I'd done it. I didn't have pushy parents, no one saying I would do it. I just felt I'd achieved it myself and it was a dream come true. People had picked up the phone and voted for me and that was enough. I don't think I slept that night, I was just in a trance, then in the morning I texted all the girls saying, "We're in the band, we ARE the band!" '

Less euphoric was Simon's former mentor Pete Waterman, who came away from the *Rivals* experience with a bad taste in his mouth. There'd been questions about the voting system and Waterman – despite claiming he'd commit suicide if they didn't get to Number 1 – had been less than enamoured of his group One True Voice.

The five lads had been living together in a shared house to supply the fly-on-the-wall aspect of the show. 'Opinions are like arseholes – everybody's got one ... And there were five arseholes in that house,' Pete later told the *Sun* in his usual diplomatic fashion. 'I should have walked out before the last night – but they talked me into doing it, and for that I'm as guilty as they are. I should have stood up and be counted but I didn't want to spoil the TV show. I didn't want to be hated. I wasn't strong enough and I wimped out. I've now learned that the truth is you've got to tell the truth.'

It looked like there was only one person who could get the British music reality show back on track: Simon Cowell. But Cowell had signed on to *American Idol* for three years, and he couldn't possibly do both.

As filming for the second series of *Idol* continued, so did Cowell's up-and-down relationship with fellow judge Paula Abdul. 'We bicker but I don't know about you but if I'm comfortable with somebody I'll argue with them,' he explained to veteran US interviewer Larry King. 'If I hate you, I'm icily polite. So, it must mean that I like her. She annoys me. She irritates me. But I couldn't do the show without her … couldn't do it.'

The contestants for the second series of *American Idol* were noticeably more prepared and professional this time around and several singers caught Simon's eye. Ruben Studdard from Alabama was an easy call – his sweet soul voice got him in and out of the audition room in double-quick time and earned him the nickname of the 'Velvet Teddy Bear'. Nerdy Clay Aiken – looking for all the world like a lab technician on his lunch break – shocked the judges with both his quiet confidence and his deep, soaring take on the Heatwave 1976 hit 'Always and Forever'. 'You don't look like a pop star,' Cowell told him, 'but you've got a great voice. So now what?' Aiken was put through.

One audition hopeful's failed attempt at impressing the judges in Miami didn't stop him going to the back of the queue and trying again. When he was turfed out by security guards he jumped on a plane, changed his hairstyle and tried again in Los Angeles. 'Everyone was weird second time around,' Cowell later commented about *American Idol 2*. 'I thought the first one was weird, but the second time around … I couldn't believe it.'

Cowell's credulity would certainly be stretched by one audition at the final stage of the try-outs in Austin, Texas. Break-dancing brothers Scottie and Jimmy Osterman signed up to strut their stuff for the judges. When nerves got the better of young Scottie the panel let him bring in his brother for moral support. The pair burst into a hip-hop version of Paula Abdul's hit 'Opposites Attract'. Only as they were reaching the end of their spirited but hopeless performance did Cowell realise that the Osterman boys were in fact Ant and Dec, who'd taken the time and trouble to fly out for a filmed stunt for their *Saturday Night Takeaway* show. Cowell would later gamely appear on the show when the stunt was broadcast on British TV. The two presenters practically wriggled with delight at getting one over on 'Old Mr High Trousers Himself'. 'This was not an unusual audition in America,' he told Ant and Dec after the prank was revealed. 'This was a good one. When you started singing I was looking over at the producer to say, "He looks like Ant, this guy." What was the giveaway was your weird dance routine.'

The Ostermans' attempt to try it on with the judges didn't get too far, and another contestant in the second series would later make a claim that his attempt was altogether more successful. One of the entrants, Corey Clark, claimed he was enjoying a sexual relationship with Paula Abdul – and that's how he made it into through in the competition. 'I have my own suspicions,' Simon told *Entertainment Weekly*. 'I wouldn't believe too much of what this guy has to say. He's after publicity for himself. He's preying on the weak. It's as simple as that. I can only say it as I saw it. Paula was much more keen to give contestants comfort afterwards. You can't condemn somebody for wanting to soothe them and make them feel better. She felt very bad if they got booted off or slighted by one of us, so she would be the first one to give them a hug or whatever afterwards, and that's all I ever saw.' Cowell's reasoning was that, at this stage of the competition, it wasn't down to the judges anyway. 'It's a show which is run by the public. In my opinion it's the only fair competition on TV at the moment. Regardless of what I say or what Paula says or what Randy says, the viewers decide who's going to stay or go.'

Clark was eventually ousted from the show because of his undisclosed police record; the claims about Abdul arose later. When Clark's allegations became public during a later series of *Idol*, the producers filmed a spoof segment in which Simon Cowell was discovered to be having an affair – with himself. It was not beyond the realms of the imagination.

With the auditions in the can, Simon took his traditional winter break, holidaying in Barbados with Nigel Lythgoe and his wife Bonnie. Stopping off in the UK on his way to the Hollywood finals, Cowell received a call that stopped him in his tracks: Nigel Lythgoe – a good old-fashioned workaholic, 60-a-day smoker – had suffered a heart attack. 'I'd just returned from a holiday in Barbados with Bonnie and Simon Cowell,' Lythgoe later revealed to the *Daily Mail*. 'I thought I had indigestion. When I went to the doctor, he called an ambulance. "But try to look a bit more ill," he said. He didn't think my tan was helping my cause.'

Doctors managed to improve the flow of blood to Lythgoe's heart, but it was still beating arrhythmically. 'So it had to be rebooted, like an old computer,' Lythgoe said. 'And that's when I cried. I'd never been so frightened.'

The heart attack was the start of a series of medical woes for the producer, who would later suffer a burst appendix and have a large part of his intestine and colon removed. But it would take more than a mere heart attack to stop Lythgoe – he was back at work three weeks later to guide the climax of *American Idol* to a showdown between soul man Ruben Studdard and dark horse Clay Aiken. Cowell would maintain that the battle between the two was one of his favourite *Idol* finals, describing it as 'the little nerd who transformed himself and the polished soul singer'. In fact, Cowell's money was on Aiken, but he was wrong, and it was Studdard who won the day after a stratospheric take on Westlife's 'Flying Without Wings'.

Despite this, Cowell has since said that Aiken was one of the programme's best ever contestants. 'Clay understood more than anyone else what made him popular and what people wanted to buy', was his appraisal for *In Touch* magazine.

Fifty million Americans had tuned into the final – half of whom picked up a phone and voted – and Simon Cowell had proved that the first success of *Idol* was no fluke. He'd taken his uncompromising style to America and had won hands down – twice. Now it was time to go back to Britain to see if lightning could strike twice there too. 'British people are very cynical,' he told Fox News. 'They cannot bear other people's success. Americans embrace other people's success. So, you've actually got it right and we've got it wrong. I was always told the American audience, they won't like that, they won't like this … it's rubbish! We like the same things, thank God. And everything here is larger than life, which I love. So it's difficult for me sometimes to go back to the UK. But it's important to go back to the UK because this is a bubble. When you're in a successful show in Hollywood, it is a bubble and then you've got to go back to the UK for reality sometimes.'

SEVEN

THE FAT LADY WINS

Simon Cowell had it made in America. He was seriously famous. Just as he had done in London in the eighties, he was in danger of taking himself very seriously indeed. 'One day in LA I turned into a self-obsessed TV arsehole,' he admitted to *OK!* magazine. 'I was looking at myself on the internet and despairing about what had been written about me. I had to say to myself: "This is fun, you are doing this for a different reason, forget about it," and I did from that moment on.'

The offers came rolling in – he did a TV ad for Vanilla Coke and was asked to appear as himself in the third instalment of the *Scary Movie* franchise, which spoofed current film trends. The films were lowbrow, unpopular with critics but highly successful; Simon would have felt right at home. Much to the joy of his many detractors, he gets blasted to death by gun-toting rappers in the movie, after he critiques their performances in a rap competition, a parody of the Eminem film *8 Mile*. The cameo was, he later admitted, a mistake: 'It was so embarrassing,' he told *Digital Spy*. 'I was very aware of other people thinking, "There's the reality TV jerk on the set of our film." I think I went too far.'

Despite the success, he wanted more. He was also working on a new dating show called *Cupid* – a sort of *Date Idol*. Would-be suitors auditioned to be a husband to 25-year-old advertising executive Lisa Shannon. Cowell was on screen as well as being the show's producer. 'I'm quite sure this show will work,' Cowell claimed in an interview with the *Los Angeles Times*. He was also preparing himself for the inevitable backlash. 'There might be harsh criticism, but, if it's deserved, then there should be. It doesn't matter, though. I see it as the critics being on one side and the audience on the other side, and I believe the audience will respond to this. One of the best things about *American Idol* is that it's opened doors that just were not open before. It's not about the limos or the autographs. I'm using my notoriety to be given a chance to be taken seriously. Within the next 48 months, I fully expect to have two or three shows on the air. Definitely.'

Defiantly touting itself as 'twisted', *Cupid* promised $1 million to Lisa Shannon and her new husband if they could stay together for a year. One TV station refused to broadcast the show, believing that it 'denigrated marriage' and the ratings weren't a patch on *Idol*; Cowell bashers took great pleasure in pointing out that *Cupid* was beaten in the ratings by repeats of a cop show. Such was the power of Simon's mojo at the time that he managed to walk away from the show unscathed.

Amid the American adventure, Simon Cowell was feeling a tug to go back home to Britain – partly through homesickness and also through a sense of duty. His American odyssey had been made possible by the faith put in him by ITV. He returned to the channel and to *Pop Idol* because he thought it was the right thing to do, despite genuine fears that he was in danger of being typecast as a panto villain. While he'd been in America, there'd been plenty of other shows to keep audiences entertained. As well as the *Popstars* reboot, the BBC had weighed in with their own version of the format with *Fame Academy*, which was essentially *Pop Idol* with all the fun and drama taken out.

In March 2003 he signed up to a second series of *Pop Idol* with the same judging panel of Waterman, Chapman and Fox accompanying him. The audition stages attracted some 20,000 contestants. With the high visibility of the first series, second-time-around *Pop Idol* seemed to attract different types of contestant from both ends of the spectrum: there were far more strong, focused vocalists with genuine ability, and there were also more delusional no-hopers, some perhaps with a view to just getting on the telly. The low quality of these contestants seemed to bring out the worst in Cowell and his reactions were even pithier than before: 'You're not good enough to be on stage, let alone a *Pop Idol*'; 'I'm just speechless – I don't know what to say because it was horrendous'; 'You are not Manchester United: you are Dagenham.'

Ant and Dec – by now experts on Cowell's critiques – were well placed to give an opinion on why Simon was so blunt with contestants. Ant: 'His excuse is, "I'm just being honest and I'm telling them what you're thinking at home." Which to a certain extent is right. At other times, he does a lot of it for effect.' Dec: 'He must lie in bed [thinking of insults] ... "I wanted a Ferrari, and you're like a Skoda – yeah, I'll keep that one." '

Cowell's descriptive powers would be tested to the limit by 22-year-old Warren Wald from north London, who barked his way through 'Eye of the Tiger' by Survivor like a wounded walrus. 'I don't think anyone in London is as bad as you, and London is a big city. Off you go. Goodbye. You find me someone in the next five hours who sings as bad as you and I'll send you to the next round.'

Wald's response to Cowell's mauling was polite bafflement: 'I've sung in public before and had a positive reaction. I felt a bit more nervous than I normally do.'

Another contestant wasn't quite so pleasant as Mr Wald. After being on the receiving end of a reasonably harsh appraisal of his singing, he dispensed with the clever wordplay and told Cowell straight: 'Simon, I think you're a complete twat and if I saw you on the street I'd quite willingly knock you out.'

In the meantime Simon was working on an upgrade to his life in London. Now that Terri Seymour was a permanent fixture on both sides of the Atlantic, he decided to move house. Holland Park, with its intimidating ex-ambassadors' residences and *Ab Fab* lifestyle, had been Cowell's home since he'd got back on his feet in the 1990s. He already had a £3.5 million pad there. But he decided to move up in the world, and splashed out on a £6 million, seven-bedroomed mansion. He then put another £750,000 into improving the house – a giant plasma screen in every room, floor-to-ceiling windows and a bright, light, slightly clinical feel to the decor. 'I'm not nostalgic about things,' he said. 'I hate belongings. I hate clutter. It really bothers me because I can't think properly. If you've got distractions in front of you, your mind goes nuts. I like things to be clean, to look nice. Then I can focus.'

One thing that would strike people as being not so nice was the way he spoke about Terri Seymour, describing her as being, 'The One – today.' He would boast of how he demanded that she refrain from asking him any questions – even to enquire about the time – after the hour of 11 o'clock. Cowell's relationship with Terri baffled outsiders: 'She goes mad when I refer to her as my current girlfriend,' he explained to the *Guardian*, 'or say: "I've never met the person I'd like to wake up with for ever." When she's upset she completely flies off the handle. I get both barrels from her and I need that.'

Seymour was asked constantly to analyse Cowell and her relationship with him: 'I don't know if I've actually tamed him,' she explained to ITV. 'I think it just works because we have so much fun. Everyone always says to me, "Is Simon as rude and obnoxious at home as he is on TV?" And I can absolutely say yes, he is. He loves the attention.'

The other issue that would come up in virtually every interview was the inevitable, coyly asked question about Simon's sexuality. Cowell's very English brand of camp, his well-groomed appearance and the amount of time he spent fussing over boy bands – well, people will talk, won't they? 'I'm used to the rumours,' Terri responded when asked the inevitable 'Is he gay?' question. 'Those stories make me laugh. He's not a rugby-playing, beer-swilling sort of guy. I think it's funny that people still say he's gay after we've been together for all this time. But it's weird. What does that mean people think he's doing with me? I don't think he cares what people think. He's never going to change to make himself appear more rugged. He'll never change anything for anyone. He's oblivious to other people's opinions.'

'If I was [gay], why hide it?' he said in an interview with the *Daily Mail*. 'It's not as if the music business would be an odd place for a gay man to work. And anyway, if I was trying to hide the fact that I was gay, I would be off playing rugby every Saturday, wouldn't I?'

Back at *Pop Idol*, the judging panel had been whittling down the list of audition hopefuls. As ever, key performers and their characters began to shine through. Chris Hide was cut from similar nerdy cloth to *American Idol*'s Clay Aiken and his earnest demeanour earned him the nickname of 'the Vicar'. Cowell didn't get him, but his strident, pleading voice wowed the other judges. Susanne Manning from Reading was an appealing mix of breathy vulnerability and talent – all the judges rated her version of 'Killing Me Softly' at the first audition, apart from Waterman: 'The lights were on, there weren't nobody home,' he decreed. From the start it was clear that nerves could be the issue for Manning. By way of contrast, Midlander Mark Rhodes and Sam Nixon from Yorkshire both had cheeky-chappiness in spades, possibly at the expense of being truly great singers. That wasn't the issue for Michelle McManus from the Glasgow suburb of Ballieston. She impressed Cowell straightaway with her powerful, ringing voice and positive attitude. But there was another issue for Michelle McManus: she was the proverbial big girl with a big personality. Because of this she seemed resigned to the fact that she was on borrowed time in the competition and she was asked on camera what she thought her chances were: 'It was always a reality that I wasn't going to be able to look like this and go very far – which is a shame, really, when you think about it, but that's just the way things are.'

Perhaps sensing another 'journey' in the way that Gareth Gates's story grabbed the public imagination, Simon became a vocal supporter of McManus throughout the competition. 'My heart goes out to her because she hasn't a chip on her shoulder,' he later explained to the *Daily Mail*. 'She never says, "I'm at a disadvantage because I'm a big girl." She just says: "My size may go against me but I've got a good voice." She hasn't moaned once and her weight has actually helped her because she stands out. You can't forget her.'

Waterman objected to her on principle: she was essentially too fat to be a pop star – end of. 'A lot of the women in pop look the same' was how McManus responded in the pages of the *Guardian*. 'They look fantastic, but they look the same – and if you don't fall into that category then you are going to stand out like a sore thumb. All the women Pete Waterman's dealt with were all similar – very small, very petite – and he's never dealt with someone like me before. But then Simon Cowell's done *American Idol* and some of the women in that were quite voluptuous, which opened his eyes. And Nicki Chapman is a woman, so she understands that, as a woman, no matter what size or shape, everyone would love to change themselves and no one is really happy with how they look. That's a part of being a woman.'

In between the initial auditions and the final 50, McManus lost two and a half stone. When she made the final cut, TV viewers saw a genuine moment between her and Cowell: as she was put through to the sing-offs she mouthed a thank-you to Simon from the stage. He acknowledged her with a nod that said: You deserved it. 'I'll sign up the winner,' Cowell said, pointing out that he was likely to get his Number 1 regardless of who won. 'So I could become very political now and be impartial, but why shouldn't I be allowed to be a Michelle fan?'

McManus, who carried herself with pride and great dignity throughout the process, was subjected to some shocking comments by the judges – and not just Pete Waterman. After she'd sung Dina Carroll's 'Don't Be a Stranger' with thrilling clarity and passion in the heat stages, Neil Fox offered this by way of feedback: 'It's a difficult one – if your record arrived at my radio station would I play it on my show? You've got a great voice – then when you see the video … who knows.'

Cowell on the other hand told McManus to believe in herself and to *be* herself: 'You came out for the first time tonight believing that you can win this competition and that's what we're looking for, belief. I think you've got that belief because you know you're a great singer ... potentially. I think you're going to breeze through this round and make the Top 10 and I want you in the Top 10 ... because I think you're great.'

The singer thanked all the judges for their comments, walked from the stage – and wept.

As the finalists began to fall by the wayside, the press pounced on a claim that the shy, retiring Susanne Manning – another Cowell favourite – was getting too big for her boots and had called Michelle a 'fat cow'. Given that McManus's profile was bordering on the saintly with the public – in Scotland she was viewed even more highly – the backlash against Manning was severe. True or not, Cowell believed that the claims caused her to exit the competition.

The live final on 20 December 2003 was all singing and dancing, an altogether slicker affair than the first final. But Cowell felt it lacked the tension and drama of the first series. Michelle went head to head with Mark Rhodes, but the combination of the McManus voice, the beguiling arc of her 'journey' and the fact that anyone in Scotland with access to a phone seemed to be on her side made the result a foregone conclusion. When Michelle was crowned the winner, Pete Waterman got up and walked out of the studio. The following day, the *News of the World* – under the headline THE FAT LADY WINS – reported how Waterman had stormed off the show denouncing the result and had refused to appear on the follow-up show on ITV2. Despite praising Michelle and the power of her voice earlier in the competition, Waterman would continue to condemn the result at every opportunity. 'She only won because she had the whole of Scotland behind her,' he raged to the *Mail on Sunday*. 'If they can vote for her as a Pop Idol, they'll vote me in as a sex god! She's just a pudding, isn't she? I still cannot understand how Simon Cowell could have said to her, "You're a breath of fresh air." '

Michelle's debut single, 'All This Time', was written by Steve Mac, Wayne Hector and Alistair Tennant. The songwriters were Cowell favourites who'd written tunes for Westlife and Five, but this song – a somewhat uninspired plodder – wasn't their best. Despite this, it duly went to Number 1 in January and stayed there for three weeks. This wasn't enough to appease Pete Waterman, who compared Michelle's sales unfavourably to the record-breaking numbers achieved by Will Young; Michelle was all part of the Simon Cowell agenda. 'The winner was rubbish and I think her low sales probably reflect that," he told *Digital Spy*. 'She won't even last six months. He [Cowell] wanted Michelle to win and she did. Will Young was a fantastic winner, Michelle is not. She is simply not a big talent and is certainly not a Pop Idol. Even the people of Scotland are bored with her.'

Waterman also took the trouble to lay into runners-up Mark Rhodes and Sam Nixon, who had teamed up as a double act: 'They're just a couple of losers. Am I being nasty there? I saw it as people just trying to make another penny out of somebody. *Pop Idol 2* was all about grabbing money. The whole series was about getting a shock result, about freaks and geeks. It wasn't about talent.'

Simon also had his concerns about *Pop Idol 2* and began

to worry that Michelle may have won through the sympathy vote. 'At the end of the second series of *Pop Idol*, I didn't know anything more about Michelle after 20 weeks than that she was overweight, came from Scotland and could belt out a song,' he explained to Scotland's *Daily Record*. 'She just had no personality. Once she came off the show, she didn't have the "X factor" required.'

If it was the X factor Simon was looking for, he decided he wasn't going to find it with the *Pop Idol* format – it had run its course and he decided that he wanted out. 'I had lost my enthusiasm,' he later wrote. 'When you are auditioning kids of a certain age it is exactly the same as fishing for cod. There comes a point where you have overfished the stocks. You have to give them time to replenish themselves. For me it had been two fun years. I was happy with my decision not to judge another series. It felt good to leave the show on a high.'

Michelle's second single was 'The Meaning of Love'; it got to Number 16 in the charts – and stalled. McManus knew her luck had run out. 'Even on the night I won, I had this feeling in the pit of my stomach,' she later told *The Times*. 'I wasn't the ideal thing as far as the makers were concerned. I was a 23-stone woman, how could they fit me into a marketing plan? Where on earth could this go? So the second single came out, there was no promotion for it. And then the chart positions came in and when it hadn't gone to Number 1 I think the record label breathed a sigh of relief. Then they fell away really quickly. It was a real "don't call us we'll call you" scenario.'

Unfortunately for Simon, there would be one more *Idol*

obligation to complete. On Christmas Day, just after the second *Pop Idol* was over, came *World Idol*. Filmed on the *Pop Idol* set, the show seemed aimed at highlighting how the *Pop Idol* concept was now a global concern by bringing winners from 11 countries together to battle it out in a Eurovision-style vote-off. Will Young represented Britain and Kelly Clarkson did her bit for the USA; both looked as if they'd rather be elsewhere. The show was won a week later by gap-toothed Norwegian Kurt Nilsen, who yodelled his way to victory with a cover of U2's 'Beautiful Day'. Given that the show went out on Christmas Day, there was a panto element to *World Idol*, with the international judges seemingly trying to outdo each other as to who could be the rudest. Cowell told Nilsen that he had 'the voice of an angel, but you look like a Hobbit'.

Nilsen was less than pleased with Cowell's comments, predicting that one day he would go too far. He told the *Daily Record*: 'What was his reason for calling me ugly? He didn't have to say it. He said it in front of everybody … 100 million people. But I don't care. At least he was bragging about my music. He liked it and said I had a good voice, so I took that in a positive way. Somebody should watch what he is saying. You never know, if he is walking down a dark alley, somebody might be waiting because he is pissed off. It won't be me, though.'

The *World Idol* concept was a nonstarter and the whole affair was an *Idol* too far. Cowell himself was not happy: 'The problem is you've got 11 winners and 10 of them are now losers,' he raged to the *New York Times*. Not only did he not like the format, he didn't think much of his fellow judges, either. 'Every one of these people has based themselves on my character,' he said. 'They think it's cool to be me.'

He particularly disapproved of Canadian judge Zack Werner. 'He doesn't know what he's talking about,' Cowell said.

Simon went on his usual exotic winter holiday to cool his heels, heading for the luxurious Sandy Lane hotel in Barbados. With its sumptuous spas, waterfalls and manicured golf courses, a night at the resort can set you back £1,300. He was snapped by the paparazzi canoodling with Terri Seymour on the beach, but what really got the tabloids excited was the revelation that the holiday was a threesome – Simon's ex-girlfriend Jackie St Clair had come along, too. 'Yes, Jackie has been with us,' Cowell confirmed to gossip columnist Richard Kay. 'We split up 20 years ago but we're best friends and she often comes on holiday with me and Terri – or whoever is my girlfriend at the time. I suppose we've done around five or six holidays together. I recommend it – it's good fun. Plus, Jackie and Terri can have a natter while I'm off on the jet-skis. And we weren't all sharing the same room, I hasten to add.'

'Jackie's always been around,' Terri explained to a baffled *Daily Mail*. 'It's not like she goes on holiday with us all the time. She came on holiday with us once because she happened to be going through a divorce at the time and Simon didn't like the idea of her being alone, which is quite thoughtful, I think. But even Simon's mother comes on holiday with us a lot, which I think is lovely.'

After his holiday threesome, Simon went straight back to

the grind of another *American Idol* – this time Series 3. Auditions took place in the usual major cities plus the new venue of Hawaii. In Texas, hopeless contestant Jonathan Rey was openly laughed at by Cowell and Jackson for his performance. 'There's not a song in the world you can sing,' Simon told him before Rey tried to throw a glass of water at the judge. If nothing else it showed that there wasn't actually Coca-Cola in Simon's ever-present Coke glass on *American Idol*. Apart from the indignity of getting soaked, the fact that Rey was able to 'attack' Cowell meant that security had become lax. 'The water thing made me realise how susceptible you are to someone actually doing something quite serious,' he told the *Mirror* back in Britain. 'You've got to be sensible about this. When you have 40 million people watching, it's not beyond reason to assume that someone may want to get on TV for all the wrong reasons.'

In San Francisco, contestant William Hung became a cult figure after his far more dignified reaction to Simon's critique of, 'You can't sing, you can't dance, so what do you want me to say?' Hung's response, 'I already gave my best, and I have no regrets at all', became a defiant catchphrase and the young student became a TV star and released an album of covers on the back of that one moment.

More seriously was a growing concern over the number of strong black singers falling by the wayside as the competition progressed. Future Oscar winner Jennifer Hudson was told by Simon she was out of her depth – and out she went. 'Simon said to me that you only get one shot at the big time,' Hudson later told E!. 'But you know what,

Simon? I got shot number two. My motto is that if you can get through *American Idol*, you can get through anything. Any time I am nervous about something I say that if I got through *Idol* I can get through anything. It helps me calm my nerves.'

Elton John – who'd been a guest judge on the show – weighed in with his opinion when asked about the voting during a press conference: 'The three people I was really impressed with – and they just happened to be black, young female singers – all seem to be landing in the bottom three. They have great voices. The fact that they're constantly in the bottom three – and I don't want to set myself up here – but I find it incredibly racist.'

Cowell was stung into making a response. He blamed what he called 'American Idles' for the singers' apparent lack of success: 'The reality is that those people simply aren't getting enough votes,' he explained to the *New York Times*. 'We have a lot of passive viewers on *American Idol* who enjoy watching, and enjoy the controversy afterwards, but don't pick up the phone.'

Cowell's comments may well have done the trick: a record-breaking 65 million people picked up their phones for Series 3. What's more, it was a black, female singer who came out on top – the explosive young gospel diva Fantasia Barrino. Cowell was a fan but was still surprised when she won: 'With Fantasia there is an element of unpredictability about her, in how she performs, in what she says when she answers you back,' he told the *New York Times*. 'There's a hint of madness there, which is good.'

Simon Cowell was now a hands-down, no-holds-barred American superstar; he'd gone way beyond cameos in *Scary Movie 3*. In February 2004 he appeared as himself in *The Simpsons*, pointing out to Homer that he had the 'talent of a dolphin'. 'It's the best thing I've ever been asked to do,' Simon said after recording the voiceover. He was a genuine American pop-culture icon – and the attention he received was overwhelming, especially from women. 'In America, you can look like Godzilla but if you're on TV you'll become attractive to women,' he revealed to the *News of the World*. 'People are obsessed with celebrity over here, much more so than in England. A girl recently came up to me in a restaurant in LA when my girlfriend Terri was sitting next to me. This girl told me she needed to ask me something privately, so I moved to her table . . . and she started to do a striptease! She got as far as undoing her shirt, then a friend of mine came over and said, "Simon, I think you'd better come back to the table." '

'In America, the women are worse,' Terri confirmed in an interview with the *Daily Mail*. 'They really have no shame as far as trying it on with Simon goes.' Terri had by now built herself a good career in America, working as a showbiz reporter for shows such as *Extra* on NBC and *Good Day Live*. 'The worst thing is when they try to be my best friend to get to him. It happens all the time, but I don't worry about it. He's famous, successful, and handsome, and so it's bound to happen.'

Not that every girl was completely won over by the Cowell charisma: 'A very, very cute girl made eye contact with me,' Simon later recalled to *The Times* about an incident during a party in America, 'walked up and whispered into my ear, "You must have a very small dick." I thought it was fantastic. There is no response to that.'

Cowell's influence was now worldwide. No market was out of bounds if he set his mind to tapping it. After being impressed by the blind Italian tenor Andrea Bocelli, whose music was used on the TV show *The Sopranos* – and by the way Bocelli was shifting albums and selling out arenas – Cowell spent two years trying to recruit members for an operatic 'man band' who could appeal to all ages and nationalities. 'I knew I didn't want female opera singers because they can sound a bit screechy, and I'd only ever seen one opera, Gilbert & Sullivan's *The Mikado*,' was Simon's reasoning behind recruiting male singers when asked by the *Daily Mail*. 'There were parts of it which were amazing and parts which were mind-numbingly boring. I wanted to like it but I couldn't. With this act I wanted to create something which, when people heard it, they would think, "What the heck was that?" and just be blown away.'

Cowell didn't personally audition the singers – he paid ten experts to find recruits for the project, dubbed Il Divo. Spanish tenor Carlos Marín was the first to be recruited: 'My manager called and said, "Simon Cowell would like to have a meeting in London," ' he told Scotland's *Sunday Mail*. 'I said, "Who is Simon Cowell?" He was unknown in Spain. I went to see him and he spent three or four days trying to convince me. Lots of people were telling me, "Carlos, you're crazy. You're going to ruin your opera career." But I decided to do it. I'm very glad I took that decision.'

When Il Divo's debut album was released in 2004, it went to Number 1 in 13 countries. 'I am more proud of this album than anything else I've ever been involved with,' Simon gushed to reporters at the album's London launch. 'Il Divo have taught me more than I have taught them. I am intimidated by and slightly in awe of their talent.'

'Simon can open doors,' admitted Marín. 'People in America were definitely curious about us because his name was attached. But he's not involved in the project day to day. And the real test is if the curiosity wears off and we still maintain people's interest.'

The curiosity about Cowell certainly hadn't worn off back in Britain and there was certainly an appetite there for more of the *Idol* format. If Cowell had indeed had his fill of *Pop Idol* he clearly hadn't let his colleagues in on his decision: 'We have already had a meeting with ITV and the production company 19 to let them know we want to host *Pop Idol* when it comes back,' Declan Donnelly told the *Sun*. 'When it's on it's the biggest show on TV – we'd be crazy to give that up. We've also had meetings with Cowell. He wants to come back in three years with *Pop Idol: The Next Generation* and blow everybody out of the water again.'

In fact, Cowell was on a 'golden handcuffs' deal with ITV, tying him exclusively to the channel in Britain. If he had an idea, it was virtually a foregone conclusion that it would find a receptive home. He did indeed have an idea for a new show. What's more, Simon wanted to make it happen under his own banner. Syco – a play on his name – had been operating under the radar since 2002. Now it was about to become one of the most famous business brands in the UK. Simon had big plans for his new project: 'This show is going to be the biggest talent search the UK has ever seen, and maybe the world has ever seen,' he told reporters at a press conference to launch his new show. 'We're trying to create a different competition, one that we haven't seen before, where 18-year-old artists will be competing against experienced older artists. People who are 35 or 36 won't take my crap. When I say they're the worst thing I've ever seen they won't say "thank you" – I'll probably get my head kicked in.'

The *X Factor* hype was up and running.

EIGHT
I DIDN'T RIP OFF ANYBODY

Simon Cowell's new format – *The X Factor* – meant that older artists could apply for the show as well as young singers and groups. And, in a twist similar to *Popstars: The Rivals*, the judges would be mentoring the acts chosen. 'The judges are in competition as well as the artists,' Cowell said. 'This time I'm going to be putting my reputation on the line as well.'

Two names that were initially in the frame to be judges on *The X Factor* were feisty former Spice Girl Mel B and Louis Walsh, manager of Westlife. 'When we started the show,' Simon later told the Biography Channel, 'I wanted to work with Louis because I'd worked with him in real life when we did Westlife for years. And, whenever we were in meetings together, no matter how serious it was, we would always laugh. He would make me laugh in the most uncomfortable situations. He'd always crack me up. I thought working with Louis on the show, it would be hysterical.'

The press were by now reporting that the team of Mel,

Louis and Simon were in place, but then another name entered the frame: Sharon Osbourne.

As a no-nonsense rock manager and promoter, Osbourne had turned around the career of her husband – former Black Sabbath frontman Ozzy Osbourne – when a combination of his behaviour and his addictions was in danger of consigning him to the 'where are they now?' bin. Sharon had overseen the rebranding of Ozzy, thanks to the Osbournes' patronage of up-and-coming bands with their Ozzfest tours and their chaotic appearances on their own MTV reality show. She was tough and loud, and swore like a pirate – here was a female judge with the potential to be even feistier than Mel B.

There was, however, one potential stumbling block: Simon had recently insulted and upset the entire Osbourne family. Ozzy had been seriously injured in a quad bike accident, and Cowell had suggested it was a publicity stunt before realising the rock star was close to death. 'I had no idea how serious Ozzy Osbourne's condition was,' he later confessed to the *Mirror*. 'I thought he'd just broken his collarbone and snapped a rib. So when I was asked on Radio 5 what I thought of Ozzy's accident I said, "Well, the good news is his record will now be a hit. Maybe it was a publicity stunt." It was a joke, but the family have gone ballistic. His wife said I should be tarred, feathered and strung up and all I cared about was success because I've no family, nobody loves me and I have nobody in my life.'

Just to add insult to injury, Cowell had also been rude about Ozzy's daughter Kelly. Simon at least had the good grace to go on Sharon's TV chat show and apologise. 'I remember her introducing me on her chat show – one of the best introductions I've had,' he confessed to the *Mirror*. 'She said: "My next guest says my daughter is a fat cow, the Osbournes are over and my husband faked injury to get a Number 1 record. Please welcome Simon Cowell!" I like her but Sharon is in a different league. She is someone you do not mess with. Big time. But there's still a good chance we'll be working together so we will see. One part of me thinks Sharon would be a great judge because she knows what she's talking about. But I'd also be a bit concerned. We've never had a great relationship. We patched it up, although I decided we wouldn't discuss my views on her daughter, Kelly.'

As it happened, Sharon Osbourne was keen to get some work quickly, as she'd just received a $2.5 million tax bill courtesy of some paperwork she'd signed years earlier relating to her father, the legendarily tough rock manager Don Arden. She needed the money and signed up for the show, but was clearly going to be no pushover: 'I've got one up on Simon and Louis – I'm the only one who has worked with a real artist. Simon has had success with two lots of puppets – Zig and Zag and the Power Rangers – and Louis is all Eurovision shit and manufactured rubbish. That's why *The X Factor* will be different – because I know what I'm talking about.'

Simon still seemed to be circling warily around Osbourne, one of the loosest cannons in the business: 'Sharon's like one of those fish at the bottom of the ocean who don't do anything till you swim near them, and then they bite you from nowhere,' he told an audience at the Edinburgh International Television Festival just before the first episode of *The X Factor* was broadcast. 'She's like a lioness because one minute she is incredibly coarse, and then, as you'll see in the first episode, she's a mum at heart. But she's dangerous, and that's what I like about her. Louis is useless, but Sharon is fantastic television.'

With Osbourne on board, there was still the matter of Spice Girl Mel B to sort out. It wouldn't be the last time that there would be something of a revolving-door policy when it came to judges on Simon's shows. The singer seemed resigned to being dropped, but seemed keen to hit Simon where it hurt: 'We have a signed agreement,' she told Sky News. 'So he will have to pay me the full fee.'

As the auditions got under way with the judging panel of Cowell, Walsh and Osbourne, it soon became clear that opening up the eligibility for entering the show was not necessarily going to increase the levels of talent. 'We had more than 50,000 entrants and there are some brilliant talents,' Simon sighed in an interview with the *Sun*. 'But there were many horrendous ones too. The auditions were the low light of the whole show for me. I'd say 90 per cent of the people who turned up were awful. We had everything from an 81-year-old granny to a 65-year-old woman trying to pass herself off as a 20-year-old. A lot of them got a dose of reality. There are more tears and tantrums on this show than I've ever seen in my life. We had security in the room – there was a lot of abuse thrown at me and people threatening all kinds of things, even to beat me up. One bloke tried to ram his Mercedes into the building after he failed his audition. It wasn't just bizarre, that's an understatement. You couldn't invent what walked through our doors.'

The thin nature of some of the talent on display at the audition stages increased the amount of 'cruel' footage for the early episodes and allowed Cowell to exercise his critique skills: 'It's like an audition for *One Flew Over the Cuckoo's Nest 2*'; 'It's the end of your singing career, that's for sure' (to one man who'd just sung 'End of My World'); 'You look like Princess Diana ... ' (to a young man named Darren).

As the *X Factor* circus continued, Simon began to spread himself very thinly. A fourth series of *American Idol* was looming, the show having settled into the American TV schedules for just after Christmas. That meant late-summer auditions in the States – all those American wannabes weren't going to audition themselves and the travelling was taking its toll. 'I do far too much flying,' Simon admitted. 'I get horrendously jetlagged. We were auditioning in San Francisco for *American Idol 4*, and I actually thought I was on *The X Factor*. For a few seconds I thought I was back in England. I suddenly remembered looking at Paula Abdul and thinking, Christ, this is the American show!'

There was also his 'day job' at BMG. The company had just announced a merger with Sony, which would make Sony BMG the second-biggest record label in the world – a busy time to be BMG's golden boy. Then there was Cowell favourites Westlife, who were experiencing a few bumps on their hitherto smooth ride with the departure of their highest-profile member Brian McFadden, who'd left to spend more time with his then wife, former Atomic Kitten Kerry Katona, and their two daughters. Westlife had vowed to continue as a four piece but they could hardly fail to notice that Simon wasn't around as much as he used to be. 'Previously he used to come down to every rehearsal we had,' Westlife's Mark Feehily recalled in the band autobiography *Our Story*. 'He looked at every jacket, every shirt, every tie, every pair of shoes, and it'd be like, "Don't like those, love them, we need to get a bit more of this … " [Now he had] become so busy with Syco and all that media empire he obviously couldn't have that level of commitment any more. Jesus, if I was Simon Cowell and I had all that, I wouldn't take time off to go and see what Westlife were wearing in a photo shoot.'

Simon also began developing a 'Business Idol' format – initially called *Mogul* – that they hoped would enjoy the same sort of success in the US as *The Apprentice*. He would need all of his business acumen in the summer of 2004, as simmering issues between him and Simon Fuller began to boil over. In July, stories about a row between BMG and 19 began spilling over from the business pages onto the front pages. Initially, the issue was whether Cowell still had the right to sign future *Idol* winners to his label. A writ was issued by Ronagold – a company set up by Cowell and BMG to exploit the *Pop Idol* artists' recordings – claiming Fuller was in breach of contract. A BMG spokesperson told industry publication *Music Week*: 'We are in dispute with 19, but we are confident we will resolve this minor dispute.'

Given that BMG were demanding an injunction against 19 Management, claiming Fuller had revoked their rights to upcoming series in the UK, America, Belgium, France, Germany, Canada, Singapore, Australia, South Africa and Poland, describing it as a 'minor dispute' could be seen as underplaying the issue a little. The press were rubbing their hands at the prospect of *The X Factor* being pushed off air if a settlement couldn't be reached, and the row looked set to be played out in the High Court in the autumn. SIMON VERSUS SIMON, the headlines screamed. The tension would be ramped up further when the tables were turned and Fuller accused Cowell of copyright infringement because of alleged similarities between *The X Factor* and *Pop Idol*. Lawyers acting for the 19 team are believed to have drawn up a list of 35 apparent similarities between the two shows, when the first episode of *The X Factor* was aired in September. The list included the style of the programme's logos, the way the show was directed and even the way presenter Kate Thornton stood outside the audition room to wait to speak to contestants.

'His [Fuller's] company says that we have ripped off *Pop Idol* with *The X Factor* – and I'm saying we didn't,' Cowell explained to *The Times*. 'These things happen all the time. He has an opinion; I have an opinion. The only thing I have to clear up is when someone says I ripped off something – then it's a personal issue. I can say to you categorically, and I can take a lie-detector test, that I didn't rip off anybody. I have to clear that up.'

Remarkably, Cowell continued working with Fuller

throughout the dispute. Even experienced business commentators were surprised at Simon's apparent ability not to allow the row to disrupt other matters: 'I'd sit down with Simon [Fuller] and we could talk about everything other than the court case. I can be incredibly detached. I can put it all down to business. Literally business.'

As ever, Max Clifford was on hand to give the press a punchy quote on the dispute: 'I'm surprised that when *Pop Idol* started they didn't get a writ from *Popstars*, *Opportunity Knocks*, *New Faces* and all the other talent shows that went before it. Whatever next? Will the BBC be getting a writ from *Coronation Street* for *EastEnders*? Historically in these situations I can't remember any case when the allegations have been successful, but I'm sure the lawyers will do very well.'

Cowell was asked by the *Financial Times* to sum up his relationship with Fuller: 'I suppose we're like brothers – and brothers squabble. We've had our squabbles and our fall-outs but I think we genuinely enjoy one another's company. We're incredibly competitive and always have been, so it was probably inevitable that at some point during *Idol* that we would split up because we're too similar.'

In fact, the Cowell-versus-Fuller row wasn't the only dispute connected with *The X Factor*. Paul Tinney from Belfast claimed he had come up with the idea for *The X Factor* three years earlier and spent £100,000 developing it, including designing a logo. 'I've invested three years of my life, not to mention a substantial sum of money, into *The X Factor*, Tinney told the *Sun*. 'I was stunned to learn that Simon Cowell had this "new" idea because it is a carbon copy of mine. I have instructed my solicitors.'

Once again, Max Clifford swung into action to put a dampener on the story on Simon's behalf: 'This whole thing was thoroughly researched and checked out by lawyers,' he said.

As the first series of *The X Factor* got into its stride, things came to a head with the Simon-versus-Simon legal wrangles. In mid-October it was announced that the first of the legal rows had been averted. The two parties managed to reach an 'amicable settlement' on the issue of signing future *Idol* winners. That still left the ongoing tussle over whether the format of *The X Factor* infringed the copyright of *Pop Idol*. Business writers predicted that the big battle between the Simons was still to come.

Meanwhile, away from the courtroom and back at the actual *X Factor* competition, the series was moving up a gear. Terri Seymour was involved, too, doing onscreen work for ITV2's *Xtra Factor* show. This time around, each of the judges was given his or her own category of act to mentor. Simon got the over-25s, who included Steve Brookstein, a soul singer with a slightly down-on-his-luck, aw-shucks demeanour, who made it through to Simon's group after initially being turned down at the audition stage. Joining him was Rowetta Satchell, the motor-mouthed former singer with Madchester legends Happy Mondays. Satchell blasted her way through the auditions, thanks largely to her force-of-nature personality. 'I turned up really drunk and did a mad audition,' she later confessed to journalist Paul Morley. 'Glad I did, because I got through. There were lots of great girl singers but I stood out because I did a really mad audition. Then I realised it's not just a music show – it's a TV show. It'd be quite boring if it was just [that] the best singer wins.'

Satchell was full of praise for Simon and his mentoring skills. Steve Brookstein was not so keen: 'Everyone thought that the artists were getting close to their mentors,' he later explained to the *Guardian*. 'I did honestly believe that Sharon did actually care for her artists to a certain degree. Whenever I saw Simon, it was literally as soon as the cameras were rolling: "Right then here we go ... here's what we're going to say ... blah, blah, thanks very much, I'm out of here." And that's my mentoring for the week. I don't think I even got close. All that time together, you're buddies and his arms are around you and you're celebrating.'

Louis, meanwhile, got the groups, featuring the gospel trio Voices With Soul and the light-opera man band G4, a sort of Home Counties version of Il Divo. Simon was able to observe how his friend handled the task of being a judge. 'Louis, when he judges, becomes a fan,' Simon commented on the documentary *In My Life*. 'It's literally like he's watching the TV at home. He's just loving it. Occasionally I've had to say to Louis, "You're not watching this at home, you have to watch it as a manager." Then he kinda focuses again. But Louis would put 9,000 people into the final, 'cos he'd just like to listen to 9,000 performances. And he'd like every single one. I have a patience span of about 30 seconds; he has about 300 years.'

Sharon got the 16–24-year-olds. Among them was Irish rocker Tabby Callaghan, who seemed to have been genetically designed to appeal to the wife of Ozzy Osbourne. Also under Sharon's wing was Cassie Compton, who was just 16 years old. Compton in particular brought out Sharon's maternal instincts. 'Right from the start, Simon told me not to get emotionally involved,' Osbourne would recall in her autobiography *Extreme*. 'But I found it increasing difficult not to, till it got to the point where I became so overprotective of the kids in my charge that, if anyone said anything against them, I'd go insane.'

To some observers, that was a fairly accurate description of what Sharon was doing anyway – the filth and the fury she poured on Cowell as the series progressed was a sight to behold. She accused Simon of editing the filmed sequences on the show so as to give his acts more airtime and make them seem more interesting and sympathetic. She was not happy about it – and, when she unhappy about something, Sharon Osbourne made Pete Waterman look like an international peace negotiator. Speaking to the *Sun*, she said: 'Simon is a complete fucker. He's a fucking wanker. I'm not going to leave the show, because I work for ITV and not for Simon. But he's fucking pissed me off. He's rigged it all.'

For good measure, she also went out of her way to accuse Simon of being 'repressed' and said he needed to 'come out'. 'Everyone knows I give out criticism on the show,' he told the *Ananova* website. 'If I give it out then I'm man enough to take it, especially from Sharon. It's nonsense – first she says I rig *The X Factor*, then I don't know talent, then I chase all the young girls. Now I'm gay. If a flood wipes out Britain next week she'll blame me for that as well.'

While Sharon's relationship with Simon seemed tainted, her dealings with one of Simon's acts, singer Steve Brookstein, would turn positively toxic as the series headed towards its pre-Christmas finale. Louis's group G4 were lined up against the singer – Walsh had already caused great offence by saying Brookstein looked like serial killer Fred West. Simon laid out the choices on offer to the public in an article for the *Sun*: 'What you have on *The X Factor* are Steve, a man whose career is in the last chance saloon, and G4, a group who are ferociously ambitious – and their lives are in *your* hands. It's the public who decide which one of these acts will win a recording contract which will change their lives for ever. You also have maturity in Steve versus youth in G4 plus the fact that these are all ordinary people who came off the street with nothing but their talent to offer. Nobody can fail to recognise the desperation each of these acts has to succeed – nor the desperation between the judges! Sharon is meant to be the impartial judge on the night. Since we all know what Sharon is like, there will no doubt be fireworks.'

Simon was alluding to an open secret on the *X Factor* set: Osbourne had taken an almost instant dislike to Steve Brookstein, compounded by what she thought was his two-faced attitude depending on whether the cameras were on or off.

During rehearsals on the night of the final, Sharon claims Brookstein was dismissive of her attempt to pay him a compliment. Sharon decided the time was right to discreetly let the singer know what she thought of him in the low-key manner the Osbournes were renowned for: 'You disrespectful piece of shit,' she screamed at him. 'You are not good enough to wash my fucking underwear. You are a talentless, worthless piece of shit and I'm going to let everybody know about you and that you are a fucking prick and a fake.'

There was pandemonium on the set as Simon and the show's producers tried to calm the situation. When the show itself was on air and it was time for the judges to make their comments about Steve's performance, all eyes turned to Sharon Osbourne: 'Listen, everybody knows the way I feel about you, Steve. I've never been a Steve fan. Steve has a very nice voice. For me he's not a superstar. And I just have to say this …' Imagine the hush in the studio gallery as the show's producers waited to hear what Sharon would say: 'I'm so fed up of Mr Humble, he's not what he seems. All that BS he gives out every week. He's full of crap and he's an average singer. Ask everyone else on this competition. He's overly confident.'

Not as bad as the mouthful she had given Brookstein earlier in the day, but it was enough to generate a cacophony of boos from the audience. 'There's an awful lot I can say,' said Cowell, trying to maintain his composure, 'but I won't. I think it was inappropriate to be personal tonight. We are very fortunate: we have careers. This is very important to him. It's about his career.'

The lines were opened and – perhaps thanks to Sharon Osbourne's rant – Steve Brookstein won the first-ever *X Factor* competition. 'She kind of knew the propaganda,' Brookstein would later reflect. 'She knew how the show was manipulated. She knew she wasn't going to win it. She knew Simon was going to win it. Sadly, because she was such a popular woman, she thought she could turn round and say anything she liked about me and the public would say, "Sharon's right." '

Brookstein released his debut single – a cover of Phil Collins's 'Against All Odds (Take a Look At Me Now)' – which debuted at Number 2 in the UK charts before rising to the top slot in the New Year. The song, an underdog's tale, fitted the story of Brookstein's 'journey' perfectly. To Cowell it also signalled the end of pop music's dominance in the chart. 'I haven't really heard a decent song for ten years' was the expert opinion he offered to the *Daily Star*. 'Pop for me is old news, it's over. I think the public want something different, which is probably why Steve Brookstein won *X Factor*. People are fed up with tacky rubbish. Look at Il Divo, look at what we've done to Westlife by them appealing to an older audience. Your average pop tunes aren't selling any more.'

It had been a baptism of fire for the first show that Simon truly called his own, but *The X Factor* was a hit. ITV had already announced plans for a second series of the show, even before the first one had finished. Whether Sharon Osbourne would be back was another matter. 'It's not up to me, is it?' she told reporters at the British Comedy Awards when asked about a possible return. 'I'm just a mere nothing who's employed by Simon. If the money's right, sure.'

To seal Simon's victory, it was quietly announced that plans for a third instalment of *Popstars* – to be called *Boy Meets Girl* and aiming to find a male–female duo – were shelved.

As usual, Simon headed for a well-earned break to Barbados at Christmas with Terri, this time taking members of his family along too, including mum Julie. He still found something to moan about in paradise: 'As soon as Terri and I woke up at 10am on Christmas Day, we opened our presents. I can't say I was overjoyed with my main present – two radio-controlled cars from my mother and Terri. It's not as though I have a secret penchant for such things. I haven't taken them out of their boxes yet. I also got some clothes including a shirt from Gucci, some picture frames, and some aftershave, typical Christmas presents, really. Because it's 80 degrees, we spent the whole day on the beach and had a traditional meal with roast turkey at a beach restaurant.'

The holiday was the perfect chance to clear his head in readiness for the fourth series of *American Idol*, which was due on air in mid-January. There was the usual hype and hoopla to accompany the series already appearing in the press. But then other stories started appearing, too. It looked as if someone, somewhere, had it in for Terri. Reports began appearing on both sides of the Atlantic that Simon wanted to end his relationship with her. Not that unusual, but a story by the *Mirror*'s gossip pages *3am* had a darker undercurrent. It suggested that Seymour had threatened to kill herself if Cowell left her. As usual in tabloid circles, the quotes came from 'pals of the couple': 'Simon wants out,' the 'insiders' claimed. 'But at the same time he doesn't want to be held responsible for something Terri might do. Every time he brings up the subject she'll say something like: "If you leave me I won't be around much longer – I can't go on without you." Or: "I won't eat anything, I'll stop eating." He's scared she might do something really silly. She's a lovely girl, but she really is at her wits' end.'

Even by the standards of the *3am* team, this was harsh stuff. The couple had been tipped off that a story was about to appear, by publicist Max Clifford. 'We were told something was going to be in the next day's papers, but Max didn't know what,' Terri later recalled to *New!* magazine. 'I phoned my mum to warn her so she was prepared. We should have spoken to Simon's mum, Julie, too. The next morning, she phoned very concerned and wondering what on earth was going on. I have never seen Simon so angry. Simon and I have no idea where the stories have come from and Simon is genuinely shocked. I don't know why people are so keen to believe we've split. I guess they hate that we're so happy together. Simon is my boyfriend and best friend. If there were any problems we would talk to each other.'

There was an immediate reaction from Simon's publicist Max Clifford: 'They're absolutely fine and getting on better than they have in a long time. They had a lovely holiday in Barbados and he's off to the States to launch the new series of *American Idol*.'

In fact, Terri flew out to America with Simon, and the pair were pounced on by reporters at the airport. 'People are jealous of Terri's success and think she's getting that only by being with me,' he told them. 'But she was successful in her own right before I came along.'

There was no doubt that the couple's relationship was fiery – to the point that things were being thrown: 'I've only done it once,' Terri explained to *Closer* magazine. 'We were on holiday and I picked up a big wooden tray and threw it at his head. He ducked – it missed. He had good reflexes. I can't even remember what caused it, something stupid. But we ended up laughing about it. I've got a very fiery temper. If something's bothering me, I'll tell him. I can rant on for ages. He hates confrontation and always turns the situation around by making me laugh. But he likes being screamed at occasionally.'

From this point onwards, the couple's relationship would be under more scrutiny than ever. Cowell would also have to deny he was up to no good at Hugh Hefner's Playboy mansion in Los Angeles. 'It was a one-second kiss,' he told *Heat* magazine. 'The girl who kissed me had a photographer with her. That's really all it was. Terri and I are in a strong relationship and nothing would jeopardise that. Of course I love all the attention – what man wouldn't? Women just come up to me and kiss me – they've even been known to put their hands down my trousers before – but Terri knows that I wouldn't do anything.'

It would not be the last time the tabloids would run negative stories about Simon and Terri's relationship. It would even be claimed that Simon was willing to pay her £1 million to end the romance.

The press pack were circling over their relationship, waiting to strike.

NINE

AS MUCH MONEY AS I CAN GET MY HANDS ON

The fourth series of *American Idol* got under way at the start of 2005 accompanied by some mind-boggling numbers. They gave a chilling indication of just how big the machine had become.

More than 33 million Americans tuned into the show – making it the most popular programme in the country apart from the Super Bowl. 'This is almost unbelievable,' Simon Fuller told Sky News. 'When TV viewers turn on in such numbers you know something special is on.' There were now 33 versions of the franchise being broadcast in 85 countries. The last series had generated $900 million in advertising, record and ticket sales in the US alone, and that included $215 million of merchandising – everything from sweets to trading cards. Cowell himself was predicting that the show could run for another ten to twenty years in America – he'd certainly signed for another five – and he was reportedly earning $8 million per season. Estimates on Cowell's American earnings would continue to rise – some reports suggested it was heading towards

$15 million a year. He seemed to have it all. He was asked by *Rolling Stone* magazine what he wanted more than anything else in the world: 'Money. As much money as I can get my hands on. It's as simple as that.'

As *USA Today* put it, 'If Idol Inc. defies the odds to stay on top, it can write the playbook on blending TV and record sales into a sustainable business.' Simon Fuller in particular was looking to the future, inventing a new way for the formula of music plus television plus internet to equal cash: 'Independent entrepreneurs can set the tone in how the 21st century might look in entertainment. I don't want to be part of the establishment. I want to create my own establishment.'

The fourth series of *American Idol* was a rather complicated affair with guest judges, rule changes and debate over the voting system. What hadn't changed was the quality and bite of the Cowell critiques: 'I think you need soul to sing that song. It's kind of like trying to have Woody Allen play the lead in *Shaft*'; 'Honestly, based on that performance, if I were sitting in the karaoke bar, I'd be switching the microphone off'; 'You have as much Latin flair as a polar bear.'

The previous season's memorably bad performance from William Hung brought some more of the odder kind of contestants out of the woodwork. By now, Cowell was wise to them and their attention-grabbing antics: 'We've had what we call "the Hung Effect" this time,' he told reporters at a press conference to launch the show. 'There's no question we've had people showing up and singing badly on purpose. They may as well have neon signs on their foreheads. That whole thing came down to one word: "naïveté". Even at the point where [Hung] got a recording contract and was talking about doing a second album, I told him, "There will be no second album." That sort of delusion was part of his charm.'

Simon spotted his favourite early in the race and stuck with her: Carrie Underwood. A wholesome countrified blonde, more American than a walking apple pie, she auditioned in St Louis with a rendition of 'I Can't Make You Love Me', a song made famous by country and western star Bonnie Raitt and a popular choice for *Idol* entrants in the States. Perhaps for this reason, Simon barely looked at the young singer during the audition. He was looking off into the distance with his arms folded. Maybe he was working out the angles; he was always looking for something different from the previous season, and perhaps Underwood was it. He later analysed what was going through his head for *Playboy* magazine: 'I was looking at Carrie purely from a marketing perspective. We needed a nice, cute, blonde middle-American country crossover artist that year, and we got it.'

In the audition itself, he put things more diplomatically: 'I'm surprised that we haven't found a good country singer yet in this competition,' Cowell told Underwood. 'I think you're very good. I think you should stay good at what you're doing as well.'

Underwood – an Oklahoma farm girl who'd never even been on a plane before – was on her way to Hollywood. 'They said around 100,000 people tried out,' Underwood would later recall in an interview with *Entertainment*

Weekly. 'For me to think that I'm one in 100,000 was ludicrous. I've always loved to sing, and I thought it would be the coolest job ever, and I thought I was OK, but there were people that were so good that made it to Hollywood Week who people never even saw.'

Back home, the stories concerning Simon's relationship with Terri Seymour again surfaced in the tabloids. In May the *News of the World* ran a piece claiming that Seymour was too obsessive, that Cowell was cheating on her and that their relationship was over. It had also become apparent that Seymour was not to be involved in the second series of *The X Factor*, adding fuel to the fire. As ever, those ever-talkative 'insiders' were on hand to provide their anonymous quotes. 'Terri is not mentioned in any of the promotional material and it seems strange she is not involved in the second series. Last time around it made perfect sense for Terri and Simon to work together so they could spend more time with each other. They were able to come to the studio every day and spend time in between shows in each other's arms. But for some reason Terri is not taking part this time and that doesn't bode well for their relationship if Simon is here in London for months on end and Terri stays over in the States, where she also works.'

The traditional denials were issued by Max Clifford, and Simon himself was prompted into a response when he was asked by the *Mirror* why Terri was not going to be part of the new series. 'She's not involved this time round because she's got too much work on,' he said. 'And, because I'm always backwards and forwards to America, I see her all the time anyway.'

Simon was indeed back in the States as the *American Idol* series headed towards its climax. The final came down to Underwood and the rockier proposition of Bo Bice, who'd got into the competition thanks to a rule change allowing people up to the age of 28 to apply. The two contrasting finalists again backed up Cowell's theory that the public were looking for something different from the competition, especially when Underwood proved to be the winner. 'I think Carrie is reflective of what's going on in this country,' Simon would later tell *Entertainment Weekly*. 'There are a lot of girls saying, "I'm bored of girls dressing like sluts. I'm bored of regressive rap lyrics. I actually just like a clean-cut girl because I'm a clean-cut girl." '

The public clearly did like this clean-cut girl – a lot. Her debut album became the fastest-selling debut by a woman in country music history, going seven times platinum. By way of contrast, though, Season Three's *Idol* winner, Fantasia Barrino, hadn't done quite so well – although her debut album sold 850,000 copies in the months after the show, it was low compared with previous winners Kelly Clarkson and Ruben Studdard. 'It's kind of mystifying what happened to Fantasia – maybe she didn't make the right record,' said Simon.

Maybe it wasn't that mystifying. Barrino herself put her finger right on the problem in an interview with *Rolling Stone*: 'Watching the show is free, and a lot of people just don't go out and buy records.'

The same problem was happening on the other side of the Atlantic.

The follow up to Steve Brookstein's debut hit was still

not forthcoming – his first album came out five months after his *X Factor* win and sold a quarter of a million copies. Not bad at all. Unfortunately for Brookstein, runners-up G4 had sold almost as many as that in their first week. The first negative comments from Cowell about Brookstein began to appear in the press. 'The irony is that Louis won, he sold a million,' he told the *Mirror*. 'So I didn't win last year, he did. Sometimes you win because you're popular. G4 came second and they sold more records.'

By summer 2005 Brookstein was dropped by Sony BMG – and he didn't go quietly. '*The X Factor* is all one big theatre – it's turning music into the WWF,' the singer told the *Daily Mail*, a barbed comment referring to Simon's past association with the world of wrestling. 'It's about killing music to make light entertainment. I've now got to break away from *The X Factor*, which is fundamentally cheese and regarded so by anyone and everyone in the industry. *The X Factor* damages your credibility – or perhaps I should say Simon Cowell does.'

Brookstein accused Cowell of not managing his career, of stifling his creativity by making him stick to cover versions and of ruining his prospects: 'In the same period last year, prior to *The X Factor*, I had performed over 200 hours of singing. This year, thanks to Simon Cowell, I've sung for a total of just 35 minutes. It's a joke. I keep asking myself what more I could have done and where I went wrong. I did everything that was asked of me – all the breakfast time TV appearances, radio tours and promotional stuff. I did my vocals for the album in two weeks. But it didn't come out for six months and I suspect that was because, after the show finished, Simon spent a month on holiday in Barbados.'

Simon was stung into a response as Brookstein's attacks were widely reported; it wasn't everyday that someone went up against Simon Cowell. 'Steve literally walked onto the show and got instant stardom,' he told the *People*. 'Life really isn't so bad for him. He won a talent show, he's had a Number 1 single, a Number 1 album. And he has the freedom now to take his career in any direction he wants. It's hardly a matter of life and death. He would never have had this opportunity without the show. Twelve months ago he could never have achieved a Number 1 single and album. I don't know what he would have done without the competition, but no one had heard of Steve Brookstein a year ago. There are thousands of artists out there who would love to have achieved what he has achieved. I can't see what he has to be disappointed about.'

Brookstein's apparent failure and the very public fallout between him and Cowell didn't stop some 75,000 people applying for the second series of *The X Factor*. Hatchets were buried, pay was negotiated and contracts were signed that meant that Louis Walsh was back on the team, as was Sharon Osbourne, despite her outlandish behaviour during the first series. Cowell admitted that the American judges were an easier proposition than their British counterparts, 'I find it easier to get on with Paula [Abdul],' he confessed to *OK! m*agazine. 'Sharon gobs off to the press the whole time. I think if you're going to say something to someone you should say it to their face. It's important that this show doesn't become about two middle-aged people having a ridiculous argument, which is what it turned into. It's got to be focused on the people who enter the competition. Otherwise it becomes a sideshow for something stupid.'

As ever, the hype and the hoopla kicked in as the *X Factor* circus came to town across Britain. The press was filled with the usual outlandish stories to stoke the fires of publicity: who was rowing with whom; what the bookies were predicting as the best bet; even that Simon's mouth had been insured in case someone punched him. All good fun – but one tale stretched the bounds of credulity to the limit: it was claimed that Cowell and Louis Walsh had gone man on man and had a fist fight backstage at the Millennium Stadium in Cardiff during the audition stages. It took four security men to prise the pair apart – apparently. 'It was crazy and we did have a huge fight,' Walsh later claimed in the *Mirror*. 'I thought he was going to kill me. We had been arguing all day about who we should let into the final stages of the show. I told Simon what I thought: that he is a huge egomaniac who doesn't know how to spot real talent. He charged into my dressing room and came for me – the next minute we were both wrestling on the floor and it all got out of hand. Simon is a big guy so I just tried to hold my own in the fight – it must have lasted about 30 seconds. He kept screaming at me, "You are going to regret this," as I shouted, "Let's sort it out once and for all." '

OK, Louis, if you say so …

In the break between the *X Factor* auditions and the live shows, Simon jetted back to the States to film the try-outs for *American Idol 5*. The travel and the schizophrenic nature of his lifestyle on two continents was clearly beginning to take its toll. 'I'm spending half my time in America and half in England, but I'm not sure for how much longer,' he admitted in an interview with the Ananova website. 'I much prefer being in England at the moment. The show's doing really well in America and I have a really good time when I'm over there, so I'd like to be there a bit longer, but come March I'll be desperate to come home.' Cowell was beginning to find that the particular brand of American super-optimism he was coming across was starting to get on his nerves. 'You know, that blinding optimism from everybody you meet.'

Perhaps to counter this, the latest batch of US auditions took place in more out-of-the-way locations, to deter 'professional auditioners'.

If he was going to find fresh talent, Simon and the *American Idol* team had to widen their reach. 'Statistically, when you look back on this show, we've probably had close to 500,000 people enter *American Idol* over the years, and to date two people look as if they are going to have careers, Carrie Underwood and Kelly Clarkson,' Simon told Hollywood.com as the process kicked in again. 'Those are horrendous statistics and they show you how difficult it is to do well in this business. That's why I say, even if you're good, it's difficult. If you're hopeless, forget it. The odds aren't great here. You just look for somebody a little bit different, really.'

Back in Britain, there was something a bit different,

characters and 'journeys' aplenty in the second *X Factor* outing – literally in the case of singing siblings Andy and Carl Pemberton, who performed under the name of Journey South. Then there was singing binman Andy Abraham – there's a great story arc if he were to win – and Welsh/Moroccan goat herder turned stripper Chico Slimani, whose hammy audition and the subsequent support of Walsh and Osbourne so appalled Simon that he walked off the judges' panel. There would even be some good old-fashioned water chucking by Osbourne, with Walsh on the receiving end after claiming Sharon had been taking 'Ozzy's drugs'. Future winner Alexandra Burke auditioned and made it to through to the edges of the final group before being dropped by Louis Walsh because he felt she wasn't ready.

Walsh's main hope was Shayne Ward, a shop worker from the tough Clayton area of Manchester who'd previously tried out for *Popstars: The Rivals*. With his sweet voice, easy manner and rough-around-the-edges good looks, Ward was like catnip to the judges and the public and he progressed with ease through the early stages. But Ward also had a grimly complex and difficult family background, and it didn't take long for the details to come out in the press. His father was in prison for rape, his older brother had been jailed for murder – though subsequently cleared – two uncles and a cousin were also in prison on murder charges and another cousin was also a convicted rapist. 'Once I got in the public eye there was no going back,' he would later tell the *Observer Music Monthly*. 'I knew that my family past would get brought up. I just thought ... that's the way it is. Because I didn't want that to get in the way of me trying my best to get on. The way I think about all this is that you've got to rise above it. I was never going to let the papers get to me.'

As the series headed towards its Christmas climax, so did another long-running and tense drama: the ongoing legal battle between the two Simons. Cowell watchers were rubbing their hands at the prospect of his fighting a multimillion-pound High Court battle with one of the few people in the world of entertainment who were richer and more powerful than he was: Simon Fuller. The claim was a straightforward one: *The X Factor* was a rip-off, a copy of *Pop Idol*.

In December it was announced that a settlement had been reached – a deal was cut at the eleventh hour. Under the terms agreed, Fuller would become part of the *X Factor* team, sharing in the success of the format. In return Cowell would get a greater slice of the action on *American Idol*, which had just been snapped up for another four series in a $70 million deal with Fox. Both men released suitably back-slapping statements about the outcome. Simon Cowell: 'I'm absolutely thrilled that we've worked out amicable terms. Simon Fuller and I have remained friends throughout this dispute and I think it was this friendship that allowed us to settle our differences in this way. We're already talking about a couple of new TV projects, which we hope to launch to the world soon. We're both happy with how this has turned out because we both gain from it. It went right up to the wire and we nearly ended up in the High Court, but we're both delighted with the outcome.'

Simon Fuller: 'Simon Cowell is a key component of the incredible success of *American Idol*. We've demonstrated that a great TV idea from the UK could take the world by storm. When Simon and I are focused and working together we're capable of great things.'

There was also an understanding declared between the two camps: that, as long as Cowell was involved in *American Idol*, he would keep *The X Factor* in Britain and not attempt to launch it in the US. The relationship between the two Simons fascinated observers: how was it possible to be embroiled in a multimillion-pound legal battle and still work together? 'Even throughout the last lawsuit, which probably lasted 18 months, we must have had dinner on five or six occasions,' Cowell explained to *Music Week*. 'I knew why he had issued us with the lawsuit and I think he knew why I had launched *X Factor*. There was a kind of understanding that only he and I understood really and, because we understand both positions, it didn't feel particularly personal. I never thought it was going to go to court, so I treated the whole thing as kind of like paperwork. We are very similar – Simon wants to be the top dog and I want to be the top dog. And I kind of like that healthy competition. He doesn't want me to be more successful than him and I don't want him to be more successful than me. I'm quite open about that. I don't have a problem with that.'

Despite just narrowly avoiding one of the biggest ever showbiz legal battles, within days of the Fuller deal being announced Simon became embroiled in another potential copyright skirmish. Cowell had been developing a celebrity singing show called *Star Duets*, and then he found out that the BBC were planning a similar show, then called *The Two of Us* – and he wasn't happy. Simon told the *Mirror*: 'We have written to the BBC that we have email proof of when we started work. We can prove we couldn't have copied theirs.'

Both sides claimed they'd been working on their shows for two years and both aimed to get them on air in the New Year. For once, Simon didn't get his way and the BBC won the tussle, and their show, eventually titled *Just the Two Us*, went ahead. Undaunted, Simon simply shifted the format to America, where it was rechristened *Celebrity Duets*.

While he was wheeling and dealing, Simon also struck a fresh deal with Sony BMG, giving the label rights to his entire roster of artists – including *X Factor* stars – for five more years. The deal covered all of Cowell's music and TV productions, as well as future projects, including any new TV shows he might become involved in.

'Simon Cowell is arguably the most important creative force in popular music television and pop music in the world, we are incredibly proud to have extended our relationship with him,' said Sony BMG's Tim Bowen. It sounded like the usual music-biz bluster – but it was probably a true reflection of Cowell's current position. Simon really was the most important figure on the global entertainment scene. Not hype – just a simple fact.

With the deals done, Simon could focus on something very important indeed – his mum Julie's eightieth birthday. In the first week of December, Cowell secretly gathered some 300 friends and family at the Savoy in London for a surprise birthday bash. He got Brendan Cole from *Strictly Come Dancing* – the BBC's rival show to *The X Factor* – to dance with Julie and she was serenaded by the cast of the West End show *The Rat Pack* accompanied by a full orchestra.

Simon might have come to regret his chumminess with *Strictly Come Dancing* – two weeks later the BBC show would beat *The X Factor* in the ratings. More than 9 million people watched Louis's act Shayne Ward triumph over Journey South and then Andy Abraham to win the series. But more than a million more would watch the *Strictly* final on the other channel. Still, nearly 11 million people voted for the *X Factor* stars that night – at 35 pence a pop, that meant more than £3 million went into the ITV and Cowell coffers. The quarter of a million copies of Shayne Ward's single that were sold in three days after the show didn't do Simon's bank balance any harm, either. Ward's song 'That's My Goal' – co-written by our old friend Jörgen Elofsson – easily topped the charts to become the Christmas Number 1. Ward took his success in a typically low-key way. 'I had no idea about this stuff back then,' he told the *Observer*. 'When someone from the record label told me how much it had sold, I said, "Oh, is that any good?" I know it was massive now, but I'm pretty much convinced that it would have sold the exact same amount of copies if it had been by Andy Abraham or Journey South.'

Ward's Number 1 crowned a stunning year for Cowell; no one could deny he was at the top of his game. It surely couldn't get any better. However, as it turned out, it could. Simon would top it with all-out assaults on TV screens on both sides of the Atlantic. But the success would bring with it huge costs on a personal level.

TEN

A SILLY LITTLE MAN

Simon Cowell seemed to be on a mission to give everyone in America the chance to make a star – or a fool – of themselves on television at the start of 2006. The *New York Daily News* put it like this: 'The surly Brit who has turned the put-down into ratings gold, is poised to become the variety show king of American television.'

As well as whittling down the finalists on the fifth series of *American Idol*, Simon was also putting would-be inventors through their paces in the multi-million-dollar *American Inventor*. The show was a million-dollar, Stars and Stripes take on the *Dragons' Den* genre. It was produced by Cowell and starred British entrepreneur and *Dragons' Den* judge Peter Jones. 'This is an exciting show,' Cowell said in a statement released to the press to publicise the show. 'Right now, someone in America may be sitting on the best new idea in the world. This show gives everyone the chance to fulfil that dream. I have no idea who or what is going to turn up, and that is the fun of this new series.'

Meanwhile as the inventions came in and *Idol* headed towards its climax, another call went out for people to come and strut their stuff for the cameras in a series of newspaper ads:

> Simon Cowell from *American Idol* is teaming up with NBC in the search for the hottest variety & novelty acts from across the country! Are you talented? Audition at one of our open calls for the chance at being Simon's next big discovery and a huge cash prize!
>
> Talents of all kinds are invited to try out. Individuals and groups welcome, singers, dancers, animal acts, bizarre novelty acts, magicians, comedians, belly dancers . . . all ages . . . the sky's the limit!! The series is scheduled to premiere this summer on NBC. Don't miss your opportunity to perform before a panel of celebrity judges on television and to prove to America *you* have what it takes to be the next big star!

To give an idea of just how wide the producers were casting their net, the application form for the show gave advice to those planning to attend the auditions: animals had to have immunisation papers, acts involving costumes had to ensure they were worn at the casting call and anyone planning to throw a knife or similar sharp object had to provide video evidence of what they were planning to do. 'We felt the time was right to open up the boundaries and say to America, regardless of what your talent is, this is a show you can enter,' Simon told reporters at a press conference to hype the programme. 'Most of the shows at the moment are either about singers or dancers or models. This is the first show that you're going to get to see literally every type of act.'

Simon also confirmed that he would be taking a backseat, off-camera role in the new show, called *America's Got Talent* – this would avoid confusion, as the show wasn't on the Fox network. It had gone through a fairly tortuous route to get to US screens. Initially created in the UK as a vehicle for Paul O'Grady, the programme was touted as a British version of *The Gong Show*, the jokily cruel American talent series from the seventies in which acts were gonged off stage when the resident judges tired of them. Unfortunately, O'Grady had a major fallout with ITV after he shifted his teatime chat show to Channel 4. The row meant that O'Grady would not be available. 'I'm not working for these petty tyrants any more,' he told the *Mirror*. 'I've told them I won't be doing Simon's show. I will lose money but I would rather be sweeping the streets than working for ITV.'

When it was decided to take the show to America, there was even talk of his moving across the Atlantic to present it and being lined up alongside former Cowell protégé David Hasselhoff. The former *Baywatch* star told CNN how he got involved: 'Simon called me up and said, "Would you do this?" And I said, "I don't want to be a judge!" And he said, "Come on, it's fun! You're funny!" Because it's Simon, I did it.'

O'Grady didn't end up being in the final line-up. When

the judging panel was actually revealed it was the curious mix of Hasselhoff, American R'n'B singer Brandy and former British tabloid editor Piers Morgan. Plummy-voiced, pompous and with a high regard for himself, Morgan immediately drew comparisons with Cowell – was he the new Simon? 'He's the new me – it's quite obvious to the audience that I'm better, I'm smarter and I'm funnier,' Piers told *Access Hollywood*. 'He promised me the next Whitney Houston, but so far the acts are less than what's expected, to put it mildly. I'm not as hard on them as Simon. He doesn't care about these people. I want them to be a great talent, but what's so sad is that some are deluded and believe they have talent worth a million dollars.'

When the series started, one US reviewer described it as a 'cavalcade of crap'. Cowell himself had to admit that the talent pool was pretty shallow in some areas – but that wasn't the point. 'We've got some amazingly good people and, frankly, some really awful people. Let's be honest. We live in a fame epidemic right now, don't we? Everyone wants to be famous.'

Hasselhoff was reportedly none too pleased with the array of ventriloquists, professional finger snappers and ageing rappers who were laid before him – and, when the Hoff is complaining about the quality of entertainment on offer, you know you've got problems. 'This is not my cup of tea,' he complained to *Newsweek* magazine. 'I signed on for one season, and Simon Cowell conned me into it. It's like *The Gong Show*.'

A spokesman for the show was quick to react and put Hasselhoff's comments 'into context': 'It was just tongue-in-cheek. David and Simon are always joking with each other. He phoned Simon and explained. He said he's very happy to be on one of America's most successful shows.'

The series was eventually won by 11-year-old singer Bianca Ryan from Philadelphia, whose career stalled shortly after the competition when her debut album managed to get only to Number 57 in the American *Billboard* charts. Ryan fared better on a new internet site that shared uploaded videos for free – her audition performance of 'And I am Telling You I am Not Going', from the musical *Showgirls*, became a massive hit on YouTube. There would be a massive appetite for videos from Cowell-related shows over the coming years and the site would play a big part in their continuing success.

Young singers were part of the Cowell plan that year. He'd sensed a gap in the market being only partially filled by Il Divo – well-packaged, easy-listening 'classical' music. He used the same technique as before: hiring experts to scour the country for the best young singers they could find. A six-strong group of 11-to-14-year-olds were assembled from the country's top choirs and Cowell christened them Angelis. 'When I first heard them sing I instinctively knew that they'd be a success,' Simon boasted to the *Daily Mail*. 'Here you have six truly gifted young people whose passion is singing – and singing well – rather than fame. In a sense it was almost the reverse of *X Factor* … we went to them.'

Unfortunately, it wasn't a deal made in heaven as far as Angelis were concerned and they lasted only a year on Simon's label before their wings were clipped. But they were an early example for what would be a mini-wave of young, classical vocal groups around this time – All Angels being a good example – and Angelis's debut album went to Number 2 in the charts. Simon had proved his point.

More young dreams were coming to an end in April as it was announced that Gareth Gates was being dropped by Sony BMG. 'The record label felt there was no way for them to take Gareth's career forward,' said a spokesman for the label in a matter-of-fact statement. 'He had been working hard on trying to relaunch himself with a new sound and new image. But his latest material wasn't strong enough to compete with fresh talent being churned out on programmes like *X Factor*.'

The faceless spokesman had pinpointed the very heart of the problem: when you've got new stars being delivered by Simon's shows on a regular basis, who needs an 'old' one? Gates, one of the very first wave of reality TV singers made famous by Simon Cowell, was 22 years old. 'Simon and I never argued,' he later insisted to the *Daily Mail*, putting a brave face on the situation. 'I had lots of success with his record company, but in truth, it wasn't as the artist I wanted to be for the rest of my life. I wanted to be happy with the music I was making – not feel a little bit embarrassed when it was on the radio. I had lots of success and lots of money in the bank, so I'm able to do what I want and have what I want. So, no, there's no real regret.'

The demise of Gareth Gates was a great excuse for Cowell bashers to put the boot into their favourite target. Simon had become such a popular culture fixture that he was now an easy target for commentators and satirists looking for a quick laugh – everybody knew who Cowell was, so it was likely that everyone would get the joke. One particular example was the Simonesque performance by Hugh Grant in the 2006 film *American Dreamz*. Grant played Martin Tweed, the vile and egotistical leading light of a TV talent show that invites the American President (Dennis Quaid) to appear as a guest judge. The film – a political satire that's nowhere near as clever as it thinks it is – was not a huge hit but at least allowed the pleasure of seeing Grant 'doing' Cowell. He studied tapes of Simon in action on his shows by way of preparation. 'I'd never watched them before but studied a bunch of tapes – and I enjoy cruelty,' Grant told ITV. 'I enjoy people being humiliated. I like watching freaks. The freakier the better as far as I'm concerned. I don't think they go far enough: I'd like to see the losers tortured. I have always had a secret desire to be on television. I like reality shows. I am a particular fan of *I'm a Celebrity . . . Get Me Out of Here!* If it wasn't beneath my dignity, I'd be doing a lot of these shows.'

Back in the 'real' world of reality TV, the fifth *American Idol* was about to be revealed. To Simon's surprise and perhaps disappointment, the winner was grey-haired soul man Taylor Hicks, who, despite being just 29, looked more like someone's dad doing a Joe Cocker impression at a party.

Cowell had felt from the start that Hicks was a 'background' singer not an Idol. Hicks was, to say the least, an unconventional winner.

The other unconventional thing about the series was the conduct of judge Paula Abdul, whose odd behaviour and out-there comments set message boards buzzing with speculation about the cause of her strange antics. Abdul blamed it on Simon playing games at the judges' table: 'He's worse than ever,' she told *In Touch Weekly*. 'If they say, "Paula is going crazy," the reason is Simon is whispering things in my ear like, "What's the price of beans?" Things that make no sense at all. Simon gave me advice and said on *The X Factor* he always refers to a fortune cookie and says, "The moth who finds the melon finds the cornflake always finds the melon and one of you didn't pick the right fortune." ' If Abdul's behaviour made no sense, her explanation made even less and speculation on the cause of her outbursts continued.

A matter of days after *American Idol 5* wrapped, Simon was back in Britain with Sharon Osbourne and Louis Walsh to do a show he would later brand as 'pointless' – *X Factor: Battle of the Stars*. The series ran over eight consecutive nights and featured a baffling mix of celebs that included rugby player Matt Stevens, Page Three girl Michelle Marsh and Radio 1 DJ Chris Moyles. 'You never know what's going to happen,' Simon told reporters at the launch of the show. 'I'm definitely going to have fun with these celebrities. We can be very cruel indeed. We need to be that bit harder on them than usual, because they're famous already.'

Former *EastEnders* actress Lucy Benjamin – who was pregnant at the time – won the competition, despite being comprehensively outperformed by Moyles. Simon decided that the show was destined to be a one-off: 'We are never going to do it again,' he told the *Sun*. 'The show was pointless. The ratings were good but what we're supposed to be looking for is a new artist. The only validity for my doing these shows is that I'm doing my day job on a TV – which is trying to find artists for the label. So when I'm judging celebs, I'm not actually doing my job. I'm just being on a TV show.'

By now, Cowell's constant jetting back and forth between London and Los Angeles had become the norm, yet he still had no real base in America. His pan-global lifestyle was now part of who he was: as well as his Holland Park home in London, he had a villa in Spain and an investment property in Dubai, and was building a house in Barbados – so there was no reason why he shouldn't have a permanent home in the US. He found a place that was partially to his liking: a $12 million mansion previously owned by Jennifer Lopez. He then promptly knocked it down and started again. 'I've been involved in every aspect of the design of the new place, right down to the doorknobs,' Cowell revealed to the *Daily Mail*. 'I have other houses but this is my dream home.'

The house would eventually boast 24-foot-high windows offering majestic views over Los Angeles and of neighbouring properties owned by the likes of Madonna, Tom Cruise and David and Victoria Beckham. The five-bedroomed house would have a spa, indoor pool, gymnasium, putting green, private cinema and tanning suite, plus separate quarters for staff and a self-contained suite for Terri Seymour. She had obviously been heavily involved in the work being done on the house – but her relationship with Simon would be fatally undermined by events that unfolded that summer.

In July the *Mirror* published a story linking Simon to 21-year-old model Jasmine Lennard. Unlike the usual tabloid nudges and winks, the *Mirror*'s piece was explicit in its allegation: Simon had been cheating on Terri Seymour for six months with Lennard, whom the paper gleefully described as a 'racy society girl'. The story went into great detail, claiming that Lennard had been spotted arriving at Cowell's Holland Park house dressed – marvellous bit of tabloid detail, this – in nothing but a fur coat and lingerie. Journalists then took huge delight in revealing details of Lennard's past, and how she'd met Cowell in a London restaurant and how he'd laid on her the classy chat-up line, 'Let's not mess about with small talk. Let's fuck.' How she'd been booted off the reality show *Make Me a Supermodel* after calling judge Rachel Hunter 'spotty, finished and fat', and had turned herself around: 'Now I'm just addicted to cigarettes, sex and sweets,' she told the *Sunday Mirror*, demonstrating her ability to provide a killer quote. 'That's what I love now – as opposed to cocaine and weed before.'

Reporters – clearly having a field day with their opportunity to make Simon squirm – even tracked down Terri Seymour's mum to put the allegations to her. 'Simon called me a couple of days ago to let me know the story was coming out,' Terri's mother Margaret told the *Mirror*. 'I just said, "Look, it's nothing to do with me. My only concern is for my daughter." He assured me I had nothing to worry about. Yes, they argued. Terri tends to get upset and fly off the handle. She seems to be dealing with it quite well. Simon likes her very much. We've met him lots of times and you can see he cares for her. She knows what he's like. She's knows he's rich and famous, she knows women throw themselves at him and that he likes it, but she trusts him. They trust each other. They've been together a long time. Terri is a one-man woman, she'd never consider cheating – not that she hasn't had lots of offers.'

The denials came thick and fast: 'These stories come out, but Jasmine is just a friend,' claimed Cowell. 'Terri has absolutely nothing to worry about.'

'It wasn't what it looked like,' said Lennard. 'Simon is a good friend, we were discussing work. We have been friends for some time.'

When Terri Seymour arrived back at Heathrow at the end of July, she was picked up at the airport by Cowell. It's claimed the pair rowed in a public area of Terminal 4 – at the height of the argument Seymour shouted at Cowell, calling him a 'silly little man' at the top of her voice.

Seymour spent the night at Holland Park, but had to brave reporters camped outside the house the following morning, telling them, 'We're still together. Everything's fine.'

As ever, 'insiders' were on hand to provide quotes for the tabloids, who kept up the pressure on Terri and Simon's relationship over the coming days: 'Jasmine has been incredibly loyal to Cowell. Publicly, she has refused to be drawn on how intimate she is with him since news of their secret affair broke. But the truth is Jasmine has deep feelings for Cowell. They have remained very close and Jasmine thinks they'd make a great couple – if Cowell wasn't with Terri.'

Lennard seemed expert when it came to fanning the flames of the story: she got a tattoo on her wrist, proudly displayed it yet coyly refused to explain the significance. The tattoo was of two letters: 'SC'.

Simon was probably glad to get back to work and got his head down with the third series of *The X Factor*. He'd just signed a deal with ITV that would keep him with the channel until at least 2008. Retaining his services was a real coup as ITV was in turmoil. Ratings for other shows were collapsing, advertising revenues were down and the defection of big stars such as Paul O'Grady wasn't helping. ITV's director of television, Simon Shaps, certainly sounded grateful when the deal was announced: 'I'm delighted that we've persuaded Simon to stay at ITV,' said Shaps. 'He is a brilliant and unique talent and I look forward to continuing to work with him both on and off screen.'

Such was his clout with ITV at this time, Cowell asked for and got a million-pound budget injection for the show, perhaps inspired by the production scale of *American Idol*. He told the *Sun* that otherwise the programme would not have returned: 'I wouldn't have worked on it unless it was going to go up a substantial gear – and that's what's going to happen. The show has got to be bigger now. We've got to make the scale of it bigger, more exciting. There are going to be some big changes on the live shows. The whole show will be rebranded.'

What stayed the same, though, was the guilty pleasure of the audition stages, with the standout being 86-year-old great grandmother Edna Moore at the Manchester try-outs. Cowell had just passed judgement on Edna's daughter-in-law Lorraine – telling the singer she was 'lifeless' and 'lacked personality'. Simon's view was: terrible. Edna was not happy and the producers, sensing a bit of TV gold, let her back into the audition room. Going right up to Cowell at the judges' table, with Simon still giggling at Lorraine's performance, Edna let rip: 'You laughed! Listen, Simon. You want to alter your ways. You think you're better than anybody. I think you were very ignorant. Yes – you were ignorant, Simon.'

Stepping outside, Edna spoke to the production team on camera and delivered the fatal blow: 'He's not good-looking. He hasn't even got his own teeth.'

Cowell was forced to admit: 'I've never been so humiliated in my life. She made me feel that big. She absolutely wiped the floor with me.'

Simon was overwhelmed by the audition stages for the third outing of the competition – some 125,000 applied. Sadly, not all of them were shining talents: 'It was like a wave of loonies this year – they just never stopped coming ... I must have said on at least ten occasions, "This has got to be a joke." But it wasn't. You put them out of your mind and you see them back on TV and think, "Christ, I remember them now." It was absolutely nonstop. I think I may have post traumatic stress disorder.'

Any stress that the wackier end of the talent pool was causing ebbed away with the arrival of Leona Lewis at the

London auditions. Despite her self-effacing manner, Lewis was a stage-school girl who had already recorded a self-funded album. Despite this background, she didn't exactly *stride* into the audition room to sing her song. 'I don't think I was that shy,' she later told the *Guardian*. 'I was more reserved and quiet. It's just the way I am. It takes me a while to come out of myself and get to know people. I am very strong in lots of ways. I'm very strong creatively, in my music. I'm very strong about the decisions I make, my ethical beliefs, and what I stand for. I think when people see that you are shy, or even just calm, collected and reserved, they think you can be pushed around, made to do everything they want – but that's definitely not true of me. The people closest to me know that's not the case. They know I'm not a pushover.'

Cowell, Osbourne and Walsh had been joined that day by guest judge Paula Abdul from *American Idol*. One by one, the judges beamed as they heard Lewis – a 21-year-old mortgage firm receptionist – soar through 'Over the Rainbow'. At the end, Cowell and Abdul both gave her a round of applause. 'That's what it's all about!' cried Simon. 'Absolutely fantastic. You're a nice girl with a great voice, you look fantastic … did it for me.'

As the first show of the series went on air, Simon appeared on the Radio 4 show *Desert Island Discs*. The programme, which has been on air since 1942, invites guests to talk about their lives and choose eight records they would take to a fictional island paradise. A invitation to appear on the programme is seen as an indication that the 'castaway' is a person of stature and worth. Eyebrows

Above: In 2007 Cowell got the red book treatment on *This is Your Life*.

Below: *American Idol* stars Randy Jackson, Paula Abdul, Ryan Seacrest and Cowell.

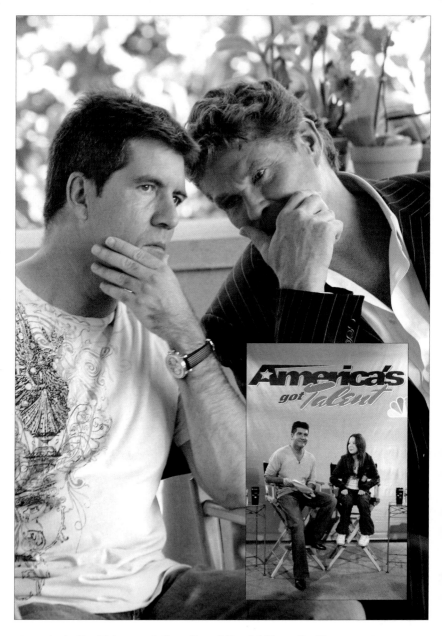

America's Got Talent and Cowell and David Hasselhoff were going
to find out where it was.   © *Rex Features*

Inset: The 2006 winner of *America's Got Talent*, Bianca Ryan, takes
questions with Simon Cowell.   © *Rex Features*

Tycoon Sir Philip Green and Cowell discussed business ventures together.

© *Rex Features*

Above: Cowell welcomes his newest judge in 2008 – Cheryl Cole.

Below: Dannii Minogue in *X Factor* mode with Cowell.

Above: *X Factor* winner Leona Lewis with Cowell.   © *Rex Features*

Below: Cowell at the 2010 *X Factor* auditions.   © *Rex Features*

Cowell out with his girlfriend Mezghan Hussainy and his mother Julie.

Above: In March 2010 Cowell faced the inquisitorial probings of fellow *Talent* judge Piers Morgan.

© *Rex Features*

Below: Cowell gets another grilling, this time from US host Jay Leno.

© *Rex Features*

The 2010 BAFTAs
included a special
award for Cowell.

© *Rex Features*

were raised when it was revealed that Cowell was to appear as a guest of presenter Sue Lawley in August 2006. Those expecting Simon to choose a list of pop fluff were surprised by the records he opted for: classic tracks by Frank Sinatra, Sammy Davis Jr and Charles Aznavour were on his list, alongside his favourite song 'Mack the Knife' by Bobby Darin. The only modern choice on Simon's list was 'If You're Not the One' by Daniel Bedingfield. Like all castaways, Simon was given the chance to take along a luxury item. His choice played precisely into the hands of Cowell bashers and is as good as example as any of Simon's brand of self-mockery: 'Easy, a mirror. It's true, because I'd miss me. I'm on my own, no one around, I might as well have a mirror.'

A few weeks later Simon had a genuine shock as he received a call telling him his beloved mum Julie had been knocked down by a car.

Initial reports suggested that she had been seriously injured after the car reversed into her, and she was taken to hospital with a suspected broken hip. Simon rushed to her bedside. 'When I heard, I was worried to death,' he told the *Sun*. 'But she's as strong as an ox and her attitude was a bit like, "What's all the fuss about?" I was obviously relieved she is fine and already planning her 100th birthday party.'

With his worries about his mum put to rest, Simon jetted to America for the next round of *American Idol* auditions before returning to Britain for the final push of *The X Factor*. Leona Lewis had sailed through the competition to come up against long-haired rocker Ben Mills and Ray Quinn, a young singer so Liverpudlian that he probably had 'cheeky Scouser' listed on his passport as his occupation. Despite Leona making it to the final, Simon was concerned that she would not go all the way and win the competition. His worry was that being female would go against her in the final. He told the *Mirror*, 'The simple fact is that girls do most of the voting and they don't tend to vote for other girls. Leona is world-class – she is the best singer we've had on *X Factor* or *Pop Idol*. She deserves to go all the way.'

She did indeed go all the way. On the night, 12.6 million people watched Leona Lewis win the third series of *The X Factor*, with some 8 million people picking up a phone to vote. Lewis's performance was also a hit on YouTube, too, with a million Americans watching her online.

Cowell had kept one piece of information from Leona that night: she was already at the centre of a bidding war between Sony and J Records, run by American record-industry legend Clive Davis, who'd worked with everyone from Aerosmith to Whitney Houston. 'Clive called me up and told me he was having a massive fight with Sony in America over who was going to get to sign Leona,' Simon later told the *Daily Mail*. 'They were at each other's throats, which I've never seen before over an artist from the UK and especially someone from a reality show. Eventually I decided to go with Clive because he said to me, "Win or lose, I'm in." And that sealed it for me. He is so confident he can make Leona a big star in America and I believe and trust him 100 per cent.'

On the night of the final a re-formed Take That – the band that Simon had passed on all those years ago – sang with the finalists. Singer Gary Barlow issued a warning to Simon Cowell: 'This girl is probably fifty times better than any other contestant you have ever had, so you have a big responsibility to make the right record with her.'

Or, put another way, you can't just use this one up and toss her aside as you have with the other acts. You have to do the right thing. You've had short-term success. People expect more, and this young woman deserves more.

After the well-publicised career collapses of Gareth Gates, Michelle McManus and Steve Brookstein, the advice from Barlow must have stung. Cowell took it on the chin and he publicly promised to do everything he could for Lewis: 'I take Gary's words very seriously. I think we have a major, major worldwide star. We're not going to make an album quickly. We're going to make the best possible album – obviously, with Leona's input, to make the album she's comfortable with. The work starts tomorrow morning on this young lady. We've got to do the job now. We're going to try to make everyone who voted for her proud that we've found a British girl who's up there with the Mariahs and the Whitneys. We take this very, very seriously.'

Cowell clearly took Barlow's words to heart: a few days later he wrote an article for the *Sun* outlining his plans for Lewis and his commitment to making things happen for her, particularly in the States. 'I'm taking her to Los Angeles to perform showcases in front of the business's biggest writers and execs. I want her to make an album that is a real statement with some brilliant songs on it. There's no need for us to rush anything, and Leona has firm ideas about the kinds of songs she wants to write and perform. She's a very talented musician, she doesn't conform to a stereotype and she knows her own mind. And I think it can only make her more endearing to the American public that she doesn't realise quite how talented she really is. America loves a rags-to-riches story – which is what Leona will have.'

Leona Lewis's debut single 'A Moment Like This' – the song made famous by Kelly Clarkson on *American Idol* – broke the world record for the fastest-selling download single, shifting 50,000 copies just half an hour after its release at midnight on the Saturday of the *X Factor* final. The success of the third series prompted ITV into beefing up their deal with Simon – he was reportedly offered £20m to keep *The X Factor* going for the next three years.

Simon admitted to the *Sun*, 'After two and half years of *The X Factor*, I'd pondered whether we were going to carry on. But this series has just been so fantastic. Leona winning means, for once, the best singer in the competition won. I think there is even more we can do with *The X Factor*.'

ITV boss Simon Shaps was asked why the deal had been offered. His answer summed up Cowell's position on both sides of the Atlantic: 'Simon's the face of the two biggest entertainment formats in the world.'

ELEVEN

WORK, MUM, WORK ...
THEN ME

As Simon Cowell and Terri Seymour headed towards their fifth anniversary as a couple, they were increasingly being asked the same question: when are you going to have kids? US chat show host Jay Leno even asked Simon live on air if he was thinking of starting a family with Terri – creating something of an awkward moment. 'We're not trying. Can we talk about *American Idol*?'

'I wish he would settle down with Terri,' his mum Julie told British gossip columnist Richard Kay. 'She's a wonderful girl. She's talented and she's good for him. They've been together for five years and I can't think of anyone who would suit him more. I've got five sons – Simon is the second youngest – and all the others are married with children. It's only natural to want the same for Simon. But you can only nag up to a point.'

Seymour admitted that Julie Cowell was probably her last hope when it came to persuading Simon to settle down: 'He might listen to her,' Terri told the *Mirror*. 'I'm under no illusion where I rank in his priorities – it's work, mum, work … then me.'

You couldn't accuse Cowell of stringing her along – again and again he'd stated that he was too old to become a father and that he was happy as he was. For the first time, Terri Seymour began to suggest that perhaps her future lay without Simon Cowell at her side. She told *Hello!* magazine, 'I've known Simon's thoughts on marriage and babies from the beginning. He doesn't want kids, full stop. But I would definitely love to have a baby. Not now, because I'm so busy. I love my job and wouldn't want to give up what I'm doing. But in the future, I definitely will. Because everything is so amazing, I haven't allowed myself to think about splitting up with Simon. Maybe I will, shortly. It's not something I'm worrying about right now. Definitely in the next couple of years though, I think it will happen.'

It was looking increasingly unlikely that Cowell's schedule would ease off in the near future. Quite the reverse. The ability of *American Idol* to get bigger and bigger astonished the US television industry. Just when they thought it couldn't get any more popular, it did. Nearly 37 million Americans tuned into the start of the sixth series – that was more than the combined totals for ABC, CBS, NBC and the CW Network. 'This is the first time in TV history that an unscripted [reality] show has grown from the fifth to sixth season – there's never been a show that dominates like *Idol*,' said industry analyst Marc Berman of *Mediaweek*. 'It's so head-and-shoulders above anything on TV right now,' he said.

But there was disquiet in some quarters that the way the show was maintaining its appeal was by being crueller to contestants. 'Sometimes we say things that maybe we shouldn't,' Simon told ABC News, 'but we're not drowning kittens.'

Newspaper columnists began to raise concerns about how the shows were being edited and the way that Ryan Seacrest tried to provoke reactions from rejected singers; there were even claims that the double door the contestants left the audition room by was locked on different sides to make the singers look foolish as they struggled to get out. There were also accusations that Cowell was ceasing to be constructive when dealing with contestants and was just being offensive. Kenneth Briggs – a slightly unfortunate-looking young man from Seattle – was humiliated by Cowell during his audition. As the cameras rolled, Simon told him, 'Your dancing is terrible, the singing was horrendous and you look like one of those creatures that live in the jungle with those massive eyes,' Simon said. 'What are they called? Bush baby.'

Simon was asked by reporters – at one of the press conferences held to promote the show – if things were going too far: 'We never try to censor the show,' he said. 'There are times, trust me, when I watch it and I say, "God, I wish I hadn't said that." I feel more comfortable being on a show where we're prepared to show the warts as well as the good things, because, truthfully, in auditions . . . bad things do happen. And I think that's why the audience trusts us because they know we will show the good things and the bad things.' Asked about the 'bush baby' incident,

Cowell said he was sorry. Sort of. 'If he's offended, then I apologise. I might never call anyone a bush baby again.'

Producers of the show later donated $1,500 to Milwaukee Zoo to sponsor a real bush baby – and had it named Simon.

While the real Simon was in the States, a row back home crossed the Atlantic in search of a quote. In March, British journalists were chasing him to find out why Louis Walsh had been sensationally axed from the forthcoming series of *The X Factor*. Such was the level of hype concerning the rows and fallouts on the show – remember that tale about Cowell and Walsh fighting in the dressing room on the previous series? – that many people assumed that the sacking was a publicity stunt. There was even talk of Louis defecting to the BBC to be a judge on the rival *Any Dream Will Do*. 'It wasn't a stunt,' Walsh later stated to the *Daily Mail*. 'But if I was on the outside looking in I would probably think it was. I was gobsmacked. I was axed from *The X Factor*, stabbed in the back. The buck stops with Simon. He hires and he fires.'

Simon claimed the decision wasn't his – odd, since *The X Factor* is made by his production company – and that he wanted Walsh to stay. 'If I was unhappy about something I would have told him to his face,' Cowell claimed after the *Mirror* tracked him down in Los Angeles. 'The truth was that at the end of last year it was all going to stay the same and I was happy with that. But at the beginning of the year ITV said they didn't want to make any decisions until early March. They came over to LA for a meeting two weeks ago and said, "We want to make a few changes." We asked for

24 hours to think it over and met again the following day. They told us it was non-negotiable. What Louis doesn't know is he had one defender in that room of seven or eight people and that was me. The only one who defended keeping him on. When Louis wants to get over this and call me and actually find out what happened, I'll tell him. I think he wants to believe there was this horrible conspiracy, that I was wielding the axe. It wasn't like that.'

Cowell has since admitted that he had one regret about the whole affair: that he did not tell Walsh himself. 'In a way I think it was a good thing for me to be sacked because in show business nothing is definite,' Louis said. 'That's a thing I always tell other people and then it happened to me. Maybe I needed that. Now I know what it's like. I had a lot of sleepless nights when I was sacked, a lot of stress, and I learned a valuable lesson. You can get a phone call that can make or break you.'

Presenter Kate Thornton also got a call – again, not from Cowell – that she too had been given the push. The fact that she was also sacked lends credence to the belief that this was no stunt. 'It was a very public sacking but it was also very private for me,' she later admitted to the *Sun*. 'I felt let down because I'd been assured privately and publicly by Simon that my job was safe. I took him at his word and he let me down. I was angry. I'd blocked out six months of my year for a job I thought was mine. I'm a freelancer and I would never, ever, judge an employer for not renewing my contract. That is their right. It's not *what* was done, it's *how* it was done. He [Cowell] called me once but I didn't return his call. I simply didn't see the point.

What would it achieve? I promised myself I wouldn't get into a war of words and I don't intend to. The people involved know how I feel. If I bump into Simon I won't feel awkward. I've done nothing wrong.'

Back on *American Idol* Paula Abdul was a source of hot debate. Some comedians were making jokes about her performance on the show. Simon offered a classic Cowellism in response: 'She's always been that way. I've *never* understood a single word she says.'

Another misunderstanding had the potential to cause even more problems for Cowell that season. On 16 April, 32 students and staff were killed and many more injured in a shooting spree at Virginia State Polytechnic and State University; it became known as the Virginia Tech Massacre, the worst case of mass shooting by a lone gunman in American history. The perpetrator, student Seung-Hui Cho, later shot himself. America's reaction to the massacre was still red raw the following night when Virginia-born *Idol* contestant Chris Richardson mentioned the killings at the end of his performance. 'My hearts and prayers go out to Virginia Tech. I have a lot of friends over there. . . . Be strong,' Richardson said on stage. The camera then cut to Cowell rolling his eyes in apparent disgust at what Richardson had just said. There was uproar as commentators condemned Cowell for the apparent disrespect he showed towards the victims. 'He would be the biggest fool on television if he did that,' executive producer Ken Warwick told reporters the following day. 'And he's not a fool, believe me.'

Cowell came out fighting: 'I've never heard so much

rubbish,' he stated. He claimed he hadn't even heard Richardson's comments and was in fact showing his exasperation with Richardson's 'nasal' performance. The audio from Cowell's microphone was even released to back up his version of events. 'I did want to clear this one up because, you know, this is a very, very sensitive subject,' Cowell said. 'The irony is that we did want to try to set the right tone on the show. And then something like this happens and it just starts fanning the flames. And people need to understand, there are families involved. It's not right. I was saying to Paula, "What does he mean, he sang nasally on purpose? I didn't understand what he was saying." So I hadn't even heard what he did. Then my eye rolled, given what I was saying to Paula.'

Cowell's explanation and the audio of what he'd actually said seemed to kill the story. As quickly as it exploded, it disappeared.

With all the uproar and misunderstanding, viewers could be forgiven for forgetting that there was also a singing competition going on. The sixth American Idol was named as Arizona teenager Jordin Sparks. At 17 she was the youngest ever Idol, perhaps tapping into the then current vogue for all things teen and wholesome, thanks to Disney's hit movie *High School Musical*.

The spring of 2007 wasn't the best of times for Simon back home. A matter of weeks after the Louis Walsh drama he had a new show on air, which aimed to find two singers to play Danny and Sandy in a new production of the musical *Grease*. From the off it didn't go down well with the critics or the public. *Grease is the Word* – produced by Syco – was unfavourably compared to the BBC hit *How Do You Solve a Problem Like Maria?*, in which the show set out to find a singer for a West End production of *The Sound of Music* under the guidance of Andrew Lloyd Webber. There has even been talk of a Cowell and Lloyd Webber collaboration on a TV talent search: 'I've known Simon for years,' Lloyd Webber told *Q* magazine in 2010. 'He's very clever and brilliant at what he does. We talked about a casting show because he could see where the music industry was going. An end game like a West End musical made sense. But we never got going.'

The overall impression of the *Grease* show was that it was a touch second-rate – the choice of judges didn't help: Cowell's pal Sinitta, *I'm a Celebrity* 'star' David Gest and highly respected but unknown American choreographer Brian Friedman. '*Grease is the Word* is not going as well as I had hoped,' Simon admitted to *Broadcast* magazine. 'It has been slaughtered by the critics – and rightly so. It is far too similar to our other formats.'

But Simon had more formats where that came from – the most obvious being *Talent*. Not content with being the face of the two biggest entertainment formats in the world, Simon decided it was time to be the face of the third. Despite David Hasselhoff's misgivings, *America's Got Talent* had been the summertime hit of the American ratings and a second series was in the pipeline. Cowell felt it was time to see if Britain had talent too. As ever, the judges were vital to the mix. Cowell – despite his already punishing schedule – decided to fill one of the places. This would ensure a quality panel, after the less-than-inspiring *Grease is the Word*.

Piers Morgan was drafted in after his success on the American version. All set to join them was Girls Aloud singer Cheryl Tweedy – now known as Cheryl Cole after her marriage the previous year to footballer Ashley Cole: 'I met Simon Cowell when I did *The Apprentice* for Comic Relief and we just clicked,' Cheryl recalled in the band biography *Dreams That Glitter*. 'That's when he decided he wanted to work with me because he liked my passion. He asked me to be a judge on *Britain's Got Talent*, but it just wasn't the right time.'

'I adored her from that moment,' Simon recalled in *Q* magazine. 'I was desperate to put her on one of my shows. I said, "Fine, I'm not going to push you into it. Having said that, I think we may have chosen the wrong show for you. Because in a year's time you're going to be working with me on *The X Factor*." She said, "I will never, ever do that show. I'm not sitting there telling people they can't sing." I said, "I'll see you in a year" and put the phone down.'

Cheryl's place was taken by actress Amanda Holden. She had been a tabloid target after her ill-fated marriage to comedian and game show host Les Dennis fell apart. Holden had engaged in a very public affair with actor Neil Morrissey and, as Morgan was formerly in charge of one of the very tabloids that had made her private life extremely public, Holden had a few choice words for him before they started.

'As soon as I met Piers, I made him apologise to me,' she explained during an interview with chat show host Michael

Parkinson. 'First of all I said, "You hounded me for three years of my life," when he was editor of the *Daily Mirror*, and that it was unnecessary and vindictive. He apologised, quite genuinely I felt, until he then said, "Of course you owe me your happiness, Amanda, because if it wasn't for me you wouldn't be happily engaged with a new baby!" '

Holden may have had misgivings about Morgan, but she had none about Simon Cowell: 'He is a pussycat. I have never seen someone with such a huge following – and obviously so successful as a man as he is at the moment – who has so much time for everybody.'

There was one person who must have been delighted by the line-up on *Britain's Got Talent*: Radio One DJ turned 'talent manager' Peter Powell. The man who had once introduced Simon Cowell as Wonder Dog on *Top of the Pops* had done pretty well for himself. His clients now included Simon Cowell, Ant and Dec and Piers Morgan. 'It's pretty amazing when he visits *Britain's Got Talent* and goes from dressing room to dressing room, because they're all on his books,' Morgan said.

Just as the series kicked in, there was a marvellously awkward moment for Simon as he was the subject of a revived version of *This Is Your Life*. Simon was surprised by Trevor McDonald at the *American Idol* finals with the guest sequences filmed later. Presenter McDonald referred to Simon as 'one of the most famous people on the planet, a visionary who has changed the landscape of television. He started out as a penniless pop music hustler ... he's now the greatest British export since the Beatles.'

If McDonald's introduction sounded gushing, that was

probably because *This Is Your Life* is an ITV programme and Cowell and his shows were currently propping up the broadcaster practically single-handedly. Simon's mum, brother, half-brothers and half-sister were there along with Ant and Dec, Randy Jackson, Paula Abdul and Ryan Seacrest. But there was one guest he wasn't expecting: the man he'd just sacked, Louis Walsh. 'This is going to be very uncomfortable,' Cowell said. Louis replied, 'Not for me!'

After a few stilted exchanges, Simon offered Walsh a 'grovelling apology' and vowed to McDonald that the pair would work again one day. 'I don't know about that,' Louis sighed.

The first series of *Britain's Got Talent* started in June and was a much more knockabout, end-of-the-pier affair than previous Cowell shows. 'Simon and Piers are just like naughty schoolboys,' Holden told the *Sun*. 'They like to wind me up. If I disagree with their verdict they say, "What do you know? You have no credibility." And I say, "So, Piers, weren't you sacked? And Simon, didn't you promote Zig and Zag?" That shuts them up! There is a real rivalry between them and they argue a lot on the show. I feel like their mother – like taking them by the scruff of the neck and saying, "Right, stop squabbling, it's straight to bed with no tea for you two." '

Viewers saw a parade of puppets, horror acts, line-dancing dogs and a woman angle grinder audition in front of the judges and a live theatre audience, but there were diamonds in the rough. Six-year-old Connie Talbot from the West Midlands was a guaranteed heart-melter, performing a perfect version of 'Over the Rainbow'.

The audience went silent as Simon delivered his verdict: 'Connie, I'm going to talk to you like an adult, OK? 'Cos I think it's important,' he said. 'I thought ... you were fantastic! I only have one question ... was that really you singing?'

The other clear stand-out came in the unlikely shape of Paul Potts, a snaggle-toothed salesman from Port Talbot in South Wales who claimed he was an opera singer. 'By day I sell mobile phones but my dream is to spend my life doing what I was born to do,' he explained. 'I've always wanted to sing as a career. Confidence has always been a difficult thing for me. I've always found it a little bit difficult being confident in myself.'

Potts's powerhouse version of 'Nessun Dorma' brought the audience to their feet and earned a round of applause from the judges. It was no surprise then to see the final being a straight fight between Potts and Connie Talbot. Morgan got a surprising glimpse of the real Simon backstage. He spotted Cowell silently patrolling the corridors, chain-smoking cigarettes. 'Don't tell me you get nervous, too,' Morgan said to his fellow judge. 'God, yes,' he replied. 'This is where you really earn your money.'

In the end it was Paul Potts who triumphed, a classic Cowell 'journey' as the underdog came out on top, especially when it was revealed that winning the show saved Potts from bankruptcy. 'I can't believe it at all,' Potts said. 'I'm like jelly. Thank you for believing in me. It's absolutely bonkers.'

Cowell told him, 'I'm so proud of you. Next week you're going to be in a recording studio making your debut album.'

The same couldn't be said of young Connie Talbot. Sony BMG pulled out of plans to make an album with her after deciding she was too young. The tabloids had a field day: 'TV's Mr Nasty Simon Cowell broke the heart of six-year-old *Britain's Got Talent* finalist Connie Talbot,' screamed the *People*, 'by going back on a vow to make her a star.' Connie's mum Sharon twisted the knife, telling the paper, 'It was a shock. Connie couldn't really understand. She asked me, "Mummy, does Simon not like me? Does he not like my singing any more?" I told her he loved her, he thought her singing was fantastic and that he would always be her best friend.'

Another 'best friend' was back on the radar towards the end of the summer: Louis Walsh. A new team had been assembled for the next round of *The X Factor*. Among them was soap actress turned pop star Dannii Minogue, who'd appeared on a TV talent show herself in Australia called *Young Talent Time*. Eyebrows were raised at Minogue's appointment – though she'd racked up an impressive number of hits in the UK. But anyone but the most ardent fan of disco pop would be hard pressed to remember any of them. She certainly wasn't known for her vocal abilities. To many she could be summed up most succinctly by three words: 'Kylie Minogue's sister'.

One person who certainly wasn't happy about Dannii's appointment was Sinitta, who had her own suggestion as to who should join the judging team: 'I would definitely be better than Dannii,' she told the *Star*. 'I don't think she takes away from the show. I just don't think she brings anything new. She's just a mini Sharon. She even looks like her. They needed a new flavour and I would have brought that. I asked Simon if I could be the fourth judge but he wouldn't let me. He said it was because he needed me to mentor his acts. He told me he couldn't do it without me, that I was Robin to his Batman.'

Sharon Osbourne hardly went out of her way to make the Australian feel welcome: 'She knows she's there because of her looks, not because of her contribution to the music industry,' she told Graham Norton on his BBC chat show. 'She's younger, she's better-looking, Simon wants her and he doesn't want me – thank God.'

Despite the misgivings, Minogue was upbeat when asked by reporters if she was looking forward to joining the show: 'I can't wait to be part of the *X Factor* team and get up close and personal on a daily basis with Simon. But he'd better watch out because when it comes to mentoring the acts the gloves will definitely be off. Just because I'm the new girl I won't be a pushover – he'll soon see my competitive streak.'

The fourth judge appointed was choreographer Brian Friedman from the ill-fated *Grease is the Word* show. Like Dannii Minogue, he was also upbeat in his press statement when the final line-up was revealed: 'I'm flattered to be offered such a coveted position. After the warm welcome the UK has already given me, I'm overjoyed to be extending my stay to work on this exciting new endeavour.'

Friedman shouldn't have bothered extending his stay by too much. No sooner had he started filming judging sequences for the programme than Louis Walsh was brought back in amid cries of 'yet another publicity stunt'.

Simon Cowell was adamant that Louis's return was for real in an interview with the *Sun*: 'Hand on heart, Louis was sacked. People keep asking if it was a scam. I wish I'd been that smart. The one thing I can tell you about the show is this: what you see is what happens. We don't censor. We don't sanitise.'

Louis made no secret of his delight at being back in the fold: 'I got called today and didn't know if it was a wind-up at first. But I'm absolutely delighted to be back. I've missed the gang, especially Sharon. Me, Simon and Sharon have a chemistry no one else has.'

But that wasn't to be the end of the controversy. After Walsh made his return to the show, Friedman was appointed 'creative director'. The shock came right in the middle of a major shake-up in the way that British television shows were being made. All programme makers were on their guard about accusations of fakery during that summer of 2007. It followed the BBC's grovelling apology over the way the Queen had been misrepresented in a short promo film aired in July for an upcoming TV series. The item made it look as if she had stormed out of a photo session with American photographer Annie Leibovitz. She hadn't – and heads rolled. 'There is this almost a paranoia at the moment with what is real and what isn't real,' Simon said when *The X Factor* got caught up in the TV fakery scare. 'If things carry on the way they are, the next time you show *Jaws* there's going to be Steven Spielberg at the top of the show saying, "By the way, the shark is made of rubber." '

Producers were forced to admit that key moments of

Walsh's return weren't quite what they seemed. ITV director of entertainment Paul Jackson admitted, 'Occasionally, we have to go back and reshoot something. We tell stories, we don't tell lies.'

Cowell said, 'If I'm honest I have missed Louis a bit and I think the show has missed him too. He is ecstatic about being back on the show. I'm sure he'll be a bit smug when he gets there but we are still looking for talent. He has a job to do.'

That job of course was ploughing through the roll call of wannabes and nevergonnabes for the audition section of the show. These included the woman named as the worst contestant ever by Simon Cowell. Rachel Lester described herself as 'better than Madonna'. 'I'm a raw talent, I've got the looks, I've got the body, I'm just too damn good – I deserve this.'

After moaning about the microphone, she proceeded to murder the Sheena Easton song 'Sugar Walls'. 'That was good, wasn't it?' she said with a smile. 'Let's face it ...' When the judges disagreed, Lester let rip: The panel were all 'cunts' and Simon's comments were 'bullshit'. 'The way you lot live your lives ... you're all fucking each other's fucking arses all to get to where you want to be. You're shit and you know you are.'

A surprisingly calm Cowell told her: 'You've got a really bad attitude, sweetheart. Everything I wouldn't want – lazy, deluded, very little talent.'

Lester was still effing and jeffing as she was escorted by security man 'Big Tony' Adkins from the audition room and then from the building altogether. Even Sharon

Osbourne was appalled – and it takes a lot to appal Sharon Osbourne. 'What an ugly, ugly person. In four years, we've never had anyone that abusive come into the room.'

In Glasgow there was an altogether more polite person to sing for the judges. Teenager Leon Jackson slid almost unnoticed into the audition room. Jackson had a strong backstory: an assistant in a clothes shop, he'd been raised by his single mum in West Lothian and had entered the competition to show her he could make something of his life. Jackson had slept rough in a car for two days before the audition and had been singing for only a matter of months. He sang 'Home' by Michael Bublé in a clear, deep voice that seemed out of place coming from his slight frame. Each positive comment that the slightly bedraggled Jackson received from the judges pushed him further to the point of tears. 'Very few people walk into this audition room with a natural talent like yours,' Simon told him. 'You've just got four yeses.'

The young Scot clearly brought out the maternal instinct in Sharon Osbourne – seeing Jackson was upset she asked who he was here with. 'I just came by myself,' he tearfully replied. There wasn't a dry eye in the house.

By way of contrast, Welsh personal trainer Rhydian Roberts entered the auditions carried aloft by a wave of self-belief and fake tan. 'I wanna be a star, I don't make any bones about that. I'm very self-confident.' Despite being baffled by his operatic voice and bullish behaviour, all the judges put him through apart from Dannii Minogue, who mimed being sick as he left the audition room. Roberts would divide opinion throughout the process, with Sharon Osbourne in particular taking against him. 'This guy is an idiot, I want to kill him! He's the most nauseating individual I've met in years. He can sing but I don't see any likeability.'

As all this was going on, the previous winner of *The X Factor* was finally emerging from her protective cocoon. Leona Lewis had seemingly disappeared after her initial *X Factor* hit. In fact she had been whisked away to work with the best songwriters, producers, stylists and media trainers in the business. In September 2007, over a year after she had first come to the public's attention she released the single 'Bleeding Love'. It went to Number 1 in 34 countries, including the US. It was quickly followed by her debut album *Spirit*, which went on to sell more than seven million copies. Cowell's strategy had worked. 'We could have rushed out a record in three months. It would have probably done a million. But you can't make an incredible record with original material in less than a year. So when everyone was saying, "What happened to Leona?" we said, "We're making the record we said we'd make." She's transcended expectations.'

September also saw Simon and Terri Seymour reach their fifth anniversary together. Seymour was asked by the *Mirror* what they had planned to mark the occasion. Unsurprisingly, the answer was, essentially, not a lot. 'Anything mushy he can't deal with,' she said. 'He couldn't bear to think we were celebrating something like that! But I'll make him take me out for dinner. I've got him trained.'

If they did go out to dinner to mark the milestone, it would be reasonable to expect Cowell to pick up the tab.

A few weeks after their anniversary, the true extent of Simon's wealth was revealed – he'd just handed over nearly £22 million in tax to the Treasury. Simon Cowell was the richest man on British television. Despite this eye-watering bill he promised he would never become a tax exile: 'I don't have a problem paying tax. I could be a tax exile, but I like living in England.'

The expectation for the final of *The X Factor* that year was that Rhydian Roberts would win. The operatic Welshman had been transformed into a bleach-blond competitive machine during the series and his opponent, Leon Jackson, was judged to be no match for his thundering voice and bombastic stage presence. Simon Cowell had made no secret of the fact that he felt Jackson was out of his depth. 'When You Believe' – a song originally written for the Disney film *The Prince of Egypt* and performed by the dream diva combination of Mariah Carey and Whitney Houston – was chosen as the winner's single. In Roberts's hands the song was overpowering and cold; Jackson's vulnerability made it achingly sad and the Scotsman won the day. When new presenter Dermot O'Leary announced that Leon had won, the teenager seemed to buckle under the enormity of what had happened to him.

Accompanied by what had now become the traditional reality show winner's video showing his 'journey' from audition hopeful to victor, Jackson's single went to Number 1, selling 275,000 copies. Unsurprisingly, Jackson – whose birthday is on 30 December – was delighted. 'I'm absolutely over the moon,' he said. 'It's the best Christmas and birthday present ever. Having the Christmas Number 1 is an amazing ending to an amazing year and I'm overwhelmed and thrilled.'

But Cowell-bashers were up in arms when they realised what this meant. It was the third year in a row that one of Simon's acts had colonised the seasonal top slot. The traditional fun of guessing who would hit Number 1 at Christmas – often accompanied by a trip down to the bookies for a flutter – had now been comprehensively spoiled. There was now no point in going up against *The X Factor* at yuletide, so no one bothered. Along with the many other reasons to hate him there was now another one: Simon Cowell had ruined Christmas.

TWELVE

YERZ DIDN'T EXPECT THAT, DID YOU?

All in all, Leon Jackson had a pretty reasonable Christmas and New Year. Simon Cowell spent his in Barbados with Terri Seymour. For a present he bought her a new Porsche. It would be their last Christmas together as a couple.

He returned to the UK to film some audition sequences for the upcoming second series of *Britain's Got Talent*, only to find himself embroiled in a bizarre spying plot. Suspicions were raised after the technical crew noticed that something was causing them sound problems on the walkie-talkie system they used to communicate at Manchester's Palace Theatre. The cause was traced to a listening device that had been planted in a green room used by Cowell, Amanda Holden and Piers Morgan. Two people were spotted listening in to the device outside the theatre. Cowell told the *Mirror*, 'I'm absolutely shocked that someone tried to bug me. It's incredible the lengths some people will go to try to get inside information about myself and the other judges. Nobody knows what they intended to do with the information they got from recording our conversations – but it is a concern that they were able to breach security.'

Security was breached again later in the year when a tracking device was found on Simon's Bentley Continental. A security sweep was ordered on his London home; theories included everything from overkeen paparazzi to betting syndicates trying to predict the outcome of his shows.

Security issues aside, Simon had a punishing schedule to look forward to in 2008: *The X Factor*, *Britain's Got Talent* and *American Idol* virtually in succession. Such was the level of commitment to his empire that he would often work till 5 o'clock in the morning. His mind was buzzing with the many projects in different continents and perhaps *American Idol* was the one giving him sleepless nights. The new series got under way and the unthinkable happened: the ratings dropped. The opening show of the seventh series was 11 per cent down on the previous season; the second night was down 18 per cent. It was still the highest-rated series on American television, but US entertainment commentators believed the show had peaked. Despite this, Fox executive Mike Darnell was upbeat: 'This show has defied gravity for so long,' he told *Variety*. 'After six years of being up every year, it's almost like it's a meaningless drop. It's such a juggernaut at this level that no one will ever want to compete with it.'

There was also concern about what had become of previous winners. While Kelly Clarkson and Carrie Underwood had gone on to great things, others hadn't fared so well. Ruben Studdard and Taylor Hicks had been dropped and the previous year's winner Jordin Sparks had turned in disappointing sales. 'It's a reflection on the unpredictability of the record business,' Cowell explained to reporters at a press conference to launch the new series. 'There's no scientific way to explain what happens. It's a reality show and what happens at the end is also reality. Am I surprised? Not particularly. The public decided it's not necessarily what they wanted, so we have to try to do better this year.'

Any US winner would be hard pressed to match the success of Britain's Leona Lewis. Her single 'Bleeding Love' topped the US *Billboard* chart in March, making her the first British female artist to reach Number 1 in the States in over twenty years. 'To say this has happened quickly is the understatement of the year,' Simon told *Digital Spy*. 'We were getting calls saying: "This record is on fire," and: "It's going to chart high." Then we got one saying: "It's gone in at Number 1." Nobody expected that. The amazing thing is I would say that 98 per cent of people in America still don't know who Leona Lewis is!'

If only all of Simon's artists were doing so well. While Leona Lewis was going from strength to strength, Shayne Ward was struggling. Talk of a big spend to launch him in America hadn't materialised and he had no new material on the horizon. Cowell didn't exactly give him a ringing endorsement when asked about Ward's future prospects: 'He's working on a new album right now, but it's up to him as to how it pans out,' Simon told Sky News. 'At *The X Factor* we give them the chance to shine. After that, they're alone.'

X Factor runner-up Rhydian Roberts was definitely not alone. The dynamic Welshman had been offered a deal by Simon straight after the finals. Cowell told *Star* magazine: 'He could make £20 million over five years. He has got something about him. He has got that look in his eyes, that steel that every good artist needs. He's a showman.'

Cowell's very open support for Roberts was seen in some quarters as a very bad sign indeed for the actual *X Factor* winner, Leon Jackson.

The sparkle that was lacking in the last series of *American Idol* would not return that season. Despite some tweaks to the format – there was a new studio set and contestants were allowed to play musical instruments if they chose to – it was hardly riveting stuff. The winner at the final show on 28 May was David Cook, a meat-and-potatoes rocker who looked unlikely to break the run of low-performing *Idol* winners to be a world beater. Despite this, the series ended on a high with a record-breaking number of viewers watching and voting.

Five days later Simon was back in the UK judging the second outing of *Britain's Got Talent*. Those with a taste for the peculiar were not disappointed by the parade of escapologists who couldn't escape, belly dancers and purveyors of 'erotic magic' who made up the talent. There were even two unlikely dancers peddling a strange mash-up of Michael Jackson and bhangra called Signature. 'We have seen some really terrible performances – worse than last year – but there have been just a few who show unexpected potential,' Simon told reporters at a press conference to launch the new series. 'In the end, it all comes down to how they manage in the live shows and what the audiences think of them. What is most important is that the winner is a deserving one. Paul Potts last year was the perfect example of what this show is all about. A guy who'd never professionally sung and who defied all the conventional rules.'

Regardless of the quality of talent on offer, the ratings were top-notch, with 14.4 million people tuning in to see 15-year-old street dancer George Sampson win the series. That was double the viewers that BBC rival *I'll Do Anything* – Andrew Lloyd Webber's search for a Nancy to star in *Oliver!* – was able to muster. Sampson scooped £100,000 and the chance to perform at the Royal Variety Show at London's Palladium Theatre. 'I'm definitely going to pay off my mum's mortgage, even though she's really independent and keeps telling me no,' Sampson told *Now* magazine after his win. 'Then I'm going to go to LA for a break, which I'm really looking forward to. I can't wait. After that, I have to practise for the Royal Variety Performance on 11 December. I'm very nervous. I don't know what I'll say to Prince Charles yet.'

As the winner was announced Simon said, 'George, let me tell you, you are the dancing version of Rocky, young man. You deserve everything because you battled your way to the top. Congratulations. The final was incredible, it was without question the closest competition I've ever judged.'

But one thing that wasn't clear was what Simon could actually do with Sampson in terms of a career after the cameras had switched off. Despite this, the teenager was upbeat about his prospects: 'I spoke to him about having a meeting this week and we're going to talk about what's happening next, so that's great. He's behind me all the way.'

A brief outbreak of Sampson-mania broke out in Britain after his win and the music he danced to on the night – a remix of 'Singin' in the Rain' by Manchester dance act Mint Royale – re-entered the charts and went to Number 1 on the strength of the massive exposure the track received. It was a Number 1 record – but neither Sampson nor Cowell could truly claim credit.

With the next series of *The X Factor* looming, there was the small matter of the judges to sort out. Negotiations with Sharon Osbourne went right down to the wire but her soured relationship with Dannii Minogue wasn't helping matters. According to Osbourne, she made the decision easy by quitting; characteristically, she didn't go quietly. 'Listen, I actually walked from *X Factor* because I couldn't stand the bullshit any more,' she told the *Sun*. 'I was getting well paid – very well paid – so it was hard to leave, but I did because they didn't like me speaking the truth. They'd rather have some doll like Dannii Minogue as judge, endorsing this bullshit. Dannii – I couldn't stand her. She wasn't so much a dim bulb as a bulb in a power cut. Fucking useless.'

Dannii Minogue commented on the backstage tension: 'I was like a scared mouse when I realised Sharon had some personal mission against me. There were a lot of days where I felt I was being bullied. It's petty and I never retaliated. I'm just so thankful it wasn't just me, Sharon and Louis, otherwise I don't think I would be going back to work. Thank God for Simon, he really did change my life.'

With Sharon gone, what Simon needed was someone with Osbourne's natural empathy with people, combined with Minogue's high-end glamour. Step forward the woman he had been trying to entice to the judges' table for the best part of two years. A gap in the Girls Aloud schedule meant that Cheryl Cole would be free. Cheryl had become the nation's sweetheart after her very public humiliation at the hands of her cheating husband, Chelsea and England footballer Ashley Cole and the pair had temporarily separated.

With just days to go before the first auditions were filmed, it was announced that Cheryl was to be the new *X Factor* judge. ITV rushed out a suitably gushing statement from the singer: 'I'm so excited to be part of such a great show and, although it's scary joining a huge programme like *The X Factor*, it's a massive honour to be following in the footsteps of Sharon Osbourne. The rest of the girls have said they're right behind me, which is really important for me as it will be weird to be on the other side of the fence this time. So, whilst we get started on the next album, it will be brilliant to be a judge on *The X Factor*.'

'She has natural instincts as to whether people are good or not, and has her own opinions. She is absolutely brilliant,' Simon told reporters at a press conference to show the press the new judging line-up. 'She is one of the best people I have ever worked with.'

Cheryl's first real hurdle was dealing not with Simon or Dannii, but with Louis Walsh. The Irishman had mentored

Cheryl as part of Girls Aloud for *Popstars: The Rivals*, but she noted that they hadn't been one of his major projects. 'I think maybe he felt a little bit guilty about Girls Aloud,' Cheryl later wrote in *Dreams That Glitter*. 'He's admitted he can't work with girls and that's okay. You can't argue with what he's achieved with Westlife and Boyzone. I don't hold grudges; what's the point? It just eats you up.'

Cheryl was in her element when dealing with the auditioning singers. Whether she was brimming with tears as she was 'blown away' by the returning Alexandra Burke or twinkling with pleasure when confronted with the four pastel-clad members of ready-made boy band JLS, there was a perfectly good reason why she was able to relate to the singers who performed for the judges. 'Out of all of the judges, I've been there and I've succeeded. I feel I can empathise with people because I've stood on that spot.'

Cheryl was adamant that, despite all her personal problems, *The X Factor* and Simon Cowell were good for her: 'Just being around Simon – and his ego – has taught me quite a lot. He's actually made me a lot more confident and a lot more comfortable. The fact that he respects me means a great deal.'

Simon and Cheryl had more in common than they thought: a running commentary on the state of her relationship had been splashed across the tabloids since January. Now it was Simon's turn.

In late spring the press rumblings began again about Simon's relationship with Terri Seymour. In April Max Clifford was once again having to swing into action to deflect rumours that the pair had split up: 'There's nothing in it, it's a rumour that's been going on for the last year or so,' Clifford told Sky News. 'It's come up now because she's buying her own place, so everybody's been sniffing around since then.'

Even the broadsheet *Daily Telegraph* was getting involved, claiming in April that Cowell had bought Seymour a £2.3 million home in Los Angeles to 'ease the pain of separation'. As ever, cue Max Clifford: 'Whether Simon helped or not, he more than likely did,' said the publicist. 'He's extremely wealthy and extremely generous, so it's reasonable to assume that he did help. It wasn't a parting gift or anything like that.'

It wasn't until November that the worst-kept secret in show business was finally confirmed. After all the denials, Clifford confirmed what everyone suspected: 'Terri phoned Simon and finished it in the September. They are going to remain close friends. Simon thinks the world of Terri and that isn't going to change. He also understands her reason for ending it.'

Terri Seymour told *Closer* magazine, 'From the beginning I knew he never wanted to get married and have kids. I've never been one of those people who dreamt of getting married, although I'd love to have a baby. I probably feel this way because my mum raised me as a single parent. Having a child with someone means more than having a marriage certificate. My clock's not ticking yet – although I'd like to have a child before I turn 40.'

Though the news was made official in November, it was clear that the pair had been apart for months. 'It happened a while ago,' Sinitta revealed to journalist Natalie Clarke. 'They'd had quite a few months to get used to it. By the time it became public, it was really old news for them.'

Newspapers columnists had a field day when the news was announced, analysing Simon and Terri's relationship down to the finest detail, with 'experts' having their say about why it had all gone wrong. Perhaps the most perceptive comment, though, came from Simon's half-sister June. To her, there was another person in his life too important to Simon for him to think about settling down: his mum. 'I have often thought that, in Simon's eyes, no woman could compete with Julie,' she told *The Daily Mail*. 'I think he has never married as he never met a woman to match her.'

One 'woman' Simon wasn't too keen on at this time was Geraldine McQueen, the trans-sexual star of *Peter Kay's Britain's Got the Pop Factor . . . and Possibly a New Celebrity Jesus Christ Soapstar Superstar Strictly on Ice*. A painstaking spoof of Simon's reality music shows, the TV show followed Geraldine's 'journey' from gender-reassigned piano player Gerry King to female superstar. On the way she fights off stiff competition from the likes of 2 Up 2 Down (a singing group featuring two performers in wheelchairs) and singer R Wayne (who was eliminated for not having a sad enough backstory – until his grandmother died). As Geraldine, Peter Kay looked like a slightly more glamorous version of Michelle McManus. To add to the authenticity of the show, former Judges Neil Fox, Nicki Chapman and Pete Waterman appeared in the show as themselves. Peter Kay even released a 'winners' single –

written by Kay and Take That's Gary Barlow – after the show. The song – called 'The Winners Song' – even had one of those uplifting key changes in it, just like the real thing. It got to Number 2 in the charts in October; Cowell wasn't impressed. 'I thought the show was clever,' he told the *Mirror* through gritted teeth. 'But the record was stupid. The single is a pathetic waste of time.'

Pete Waterman seemed to have taken great pleasure in sending up the whole process: 'Simon doesn't have a sense of humour – we're best mates but he's fallen out with me. I rang Simon so he could say, "Your comedy acting is genius, Pete." But it seems he doesn't think it's at all funny.'

Meanwhile, the real thing was heading towards the live final shows; it may not have been as funny as Peter Kay's version, but *The X Factor* was clearly developing into a far more entertaining battle than its rather dry American counterpart. The fifth series had a competitor to suit all tastes: the exotic sex appeal of Spanish-born Ruth Lorenzo, fluttery indie-chick Diana Vickers, bogbrush-haired teen idol Eoghan Quigg, dramatic diva Alexandra Burke and the jack-the-lad swing of JLS. Simon's pulling power drew a fearsome array of artists to appear on the show alongside the contestants too: Take That, Miley Cyrus and a rather confused-looking Britney Spears all appeared on the show. Beyoncé Knowles sang with Cheryl Cole's act Alexandra Burke in a show-stopping moment that may well have helped seal the young Londoner's victory. When she was crowned winner, the hyper-emotional Burke was overcome. 'It was really emotional seeing Alexandra Burke win,' said Cole. 'She's an amazing talent and has worked so hard. It was a joy to mentor her and see her grow in confidence week by week. When the series began she was one of thousands of people auditioning and in the space of a few weeks she was on stage with Beyoncé.'

Alexandra – who had oozed positivity throughout the series – had a clear message for Simon after the show was over: 'I literally said to him: "I don't want breaks, don't give me breaks!" ' she told MTV. 'Christmas will be my break – 25th of December – then, apart from that, I don't want a break: I want to work, I want a gig, I just want to sing. This is my chance, no distractions, come on!'

Mentor Cheryl Cole had her own advice for Burke, perhaps born of her own experiences that year: 'No distractions, she said. She was like, "Keep men well out of the way." And it's quite crazy because I've always had a distraction in my life and now I've not – I just want to concentrate now. This is it for me and I want to make this work.'

The winning single was a odd choice: instead of the usual uplifting Anglo-Scandinavian ballad, Burke's song was 'Hallelujah', written and recorded by downbeat troubadour Leonard Cohen in 1984. The song – filled with fevered Biblical references – had been a popular cover version of choice for artists such as Bob Dylan, Rufus Wainwright and Jeff Buckley, who died in 1997. The Buckley version became the focus of an early example of an internet-based effort to keep a Cowell act off the Christmas Number 1 spot. A variety of unconnected Facebook sites popped up simultaneously to push the idea of buying the Buckley track instead of the Alexandra Burke version. It was good enough to get Buckley to Number 2, but wilted in the face of Burke's chart assault as she sold more than 100,000 copies on download on the first day of release, more than half a million by the end of the week and well over a million in total. Leonard Cohen's version even charted – a lowly Number 36 – but Len was still laughing all the way to the bank.

But, then again, so was Simon Cowell. As he headed into the New Year and a new season of *American Idol*, he did so in pole position – he was the highest-paid man on American television. Unfortunately, he wasn't the happiest. He was bored with *American Idol* and he was bored with the people entering. 'They were so media-savvy, these contestants, that they never really showed us their true personalities – they were like robots,' he told the *New York Daily Post*. 'I didn't know much more about them at the end than I did in the beginning. I think the talent was great, and the ratings were great. I think that it could be more interesting and controversial than it was last year – you're definitely going to see a change and I think it will be an improvement.'

One change was the departure of Nigel Lythgoe, who left to concentrate on his other show, *So You Think You Can Dance?* 'I don't think we would have had the success we initially had without Nigel,' Cowell said, 'but I think that it feels like it's going to be a different show this year and we'll have to see if that's a negative or an advantage.'

One shocking incident during the series was certainly more different than anyone could have imagined. On 11 November, a former *American Idol* contestant, Paula

Goodspeed, was found dead in a car close to Paula Abdul's home in Los Angeles. Police said that prescription pills, along with CDs and pictures of Abdul, were found in the car with her. 'It was devastating and tragic, and there aren't enough feelings that I can articulate without getting into a whole plethora of things,' Abdul told *Good Morning America* several weeks later. 'I've got to tell you, luckily for me, I was at Hollywood Week for *American Idol* when it happened. I can't even imagine if I was right there in my home. It's just been a very, very tough three weeks for me . . . and for her family and for everyone involved.'

Goodspeed had auditioned for *Idol* in 2005 and the footage had been largely used for comic effect, with Simon in particular mocking the sizable braces on her teeth. 'I don't think any artist on earth could sing with that much metal in your mouth . . . that's like a bridge. How did she get through the metal detector? It must have gone crazy.'

Sonja McIntyre, Goodspeed's niece, told US television, 'Saying that she had a bridge in her mouth? That's rude. She didn't go there for looks: she went there for vocals, she went there to sing.'

When her appearance on the show was broadcast, Goodspeed wrote on her MySpace site that she was finding things difficult, because of the 'haters'. Her death opened up the debate on whether the judges, particularly Simon Cowell, were too harsh on contestants and too personal in their comments. Was it time for a rethink? 'I don't think Simon Cowell will rethink anything,' Abdul said. 'He's a man that marches to the beat of his own drum.'

There were changes to the format of *American Idol*, but

they were for cosmetic and entertainment purposes only. There was a larger pool of 36 semi-finalists to choose from and the judges were able to stop one contestant being eliminated at the eleventh hour. Studio performances would appear on the iTunes rankings and the winner would be appearing on the new *American Idol* Experience attraction at Disney World in Florida. Also, there was a new judge in the glamorous shape of songwriter and producer Kara DioGuardi, who'd worked with the likes of Kelly Clarkson, Christina Aguilera and Pink and was fully aware that she had an uphill task ahead of her. 'You're joining a team of three judges that have been together for seven years,' she told MTV. 'They're very close and they've been incredible at their job – they've made the show number one. I'm hoping that America will accept me and they'll think that I have something to bring to the table, because I feel I do.'

DioGuardi had worked with Abdul before, co-writing a song called 'Spinning Around' with her. Simon Cowell was more of an unknown quantity: 'Simon I knew *of* . . . I did not know *him*. Now I know him *well*,' she said, diplomatically.

It was hoped that the addition of DioGuardi, with her striking looks and heavyweight music credentials, plus the format tweaks, would help the show to be less dry than last year. As it happened, the eighth series was effectively energised by one man: Adam Lambert. An experienced stage performer from Indianapolis, Lambert was described by Simon at his audition as 'theatrical' – which was something of an understatement. With his up-to-the-minute haircut and camp demeanour, he was a dramatic enough performer to hold his own with makeup-plastered shock rockers Kiss on one of the live knockout shows and inventive enough to get a standing ovation from Simon with his take on 'Mad World' by Tears for Fears.

The series finale was marred by a bizarre incident outside the theatre where the show was taking place, when Terri Seymour was attacked by a crazed Paula Abdul fan. The well-built woman – later named by police as 33-year-old Janice Thibodeaux – grabbed Seymour from behind, claiming she was acting in revenge after Simon had jokingly pretended to throttle Abdul during a previous show. 'It was all so sudden – very scary,' Seymour said. 'Nothing like this has ever happened to me before. She came over to me and said, "You're that girl from TV, right?" And I said, "Yeah" . . . The next thing I know, this woman had me in a headlock and tried to choke me.'

'I wasn't cool with Simon Cowell choking Paula Abdul on the show last week and with her crying out "help" as he did so," Thibodeaux told the *Radaronline* website after she was arrested. 'Nobody said anything about that so I wanted to confront him about it because that is not appropriate behaviour, is it? She [Seymour] was taking some photographs with her camera and I knew she was his girlfriend so I went up to her to tell her how I felt. We started arguing and then I put my hands around her neck and started choking her just like Simon had done with Paula. Then I walked away and I was tackled by the police, but I don't regret what I did because of what Simon did to Paula, nobody seemed to care about that.'

After the attack it's believed Simon diverted his

bodyguards to watch over Seymour during the rest of the show while she filed reports for the TV show *Extra*.

When nearly 100 million Americans voted in the *American Idol* final and Lambert came second, even winner Kris Allen said that Lambert deserved to win. And it was Lambert who was asked to appear on the cover of America's influential *Rolling Stone* magazine after the competition, not Allen. Lambert used the article to confirm what everyone in the US had already figured out – that he was gay and that it probably cost him the *American Idol* title. 'I don't think it should be a surprise for anyone to hear that I'm gay, I'm proud of my sexuality,' Lambert told the magazine. 'I embrace it. It's just another part of me. But I'm trying to be a singer, not a civil rights leader.'

By way of contrast 23-year-old Allen – the first married Idol – said he wanted to spend more time with his wife. It didn't take long for Cowell to start talking Allen down. 'Kris is probably the right winner in terms of being a nice guy,' Cowell told Ryan Seacrest on the *Idol* host's syndicated radio show. 'Was he the best singer in the competition? No. I mean he's popular. If you allow America to vote, you live with the vote. I wouldn't have said he was the best singer in the competition, no. He was like a little puppy dog.'

This was the latest – and so far most dramatic – case of a runner-up outstripping the winner in one of Simon's shows. It was becoming a regular feature: in March former *X Factor* winner Leon Jackson was dropped by Syco. The young singer found out about it by reading it in the paper. 'Word filtered through the management about the likelihood of it happening but I was never told a date,' he told Scotland's *Daily Record*. 'No one at the label ever told me. I'm happy and not at all bitter. I think, in fact, this could be a blessing in disguise. It's evident that I wasn't Simon Cowell's favourite choice to win *X Factor*. Simon said that Rhydian should have won it. Other people have made out that I deserved to be dropped by comparing my sales to those of Rhydian, saying I sold a mere 130,000 records compared to Rhydian's 500,000 albums.'

As Jackson licked his wounds, the new series of *Britain's Got Talent* had started, kicking off with a good old-fashioned backstage argy-bargy. The show's schedule wasn't ideal – it clashed with the end of the *American Idol* run and Cowell was criss-crossing the Atlantic to fulfil both commitments. Simon had brought in former model and *Big Breakfast* presenter Kelly Brook, perhaps believing she could 'do a Cheryl Cole' and boost the glamour and emotion levels on the show. Presenters Ant and Dec weren't happy that – according to their autobiography – Brook asked them what they did on the show. She was off the programme after barely a week. 'Basically, I just don't think Ant and Dec liked me,' she later told the *Daily Mail*. 'Their egos are such that they were saying to themselves, "How dare she think she can come on to *our* show?", and since then they've been very vocal about their displeasure at me being there. I have to say it's the first experience I have had of that kind of behaviour and I was shocked by it, actually. Of course, Simon was oblivious to it all because he was off doing *American Idol* at the same time. But I have seen him since and he told me that if it had been down to him I would have still been on the show because he thought I was great. He actually said, "You don't even want to know what was going on behind the scenes. It is just a case of some people not wanting you there." '

Away from the backstage drama, there was a talent competition to run. Street dancers, fruit jugglers, drag acts and opera-singing flower-arrangers were on hand to do their stuff to varying degrees of success in front of the judges and several thousand members of the audience. At the Glasgow leg of the auditions, one of the wannabes was picked out by producers as worth a visit from the film crew plus presenters Ant and Dec. She was first seen munching on a sandwich that she'd made for the journey from the town of Blackburn, West Lothian. Looking like the spinster aunt that you dread having to kiss at Christmas, the woman introduced herself to Ant and Dec in the waiting room: 'My name is Susan Boyle. I'm nearly 48. Currently unemployed but still looking … and I'm going to sing for you on *Britain's Got Talent* tonight. At the moment I live on my own with my cat called Pebbles, but I've never been married … never been kissed … Oh shame! But that's not an advert. I've always wanted to perform in front of a large audience. I'm going to make that audience rock!'

The 3,000-strong audience at the Scotttish Exhibition and Conference Centre (SECC) on the banks of the River Clyde probably weren't expecting to rock when the woman walked out on stage with her hand jauntily placed on her hip. They were more likely expecting a good laugh at her expense. She got cruel wolf whistles when she told the panel how old she was and a horrified wave of laughter when she rather bafflingly decided to grind her hips in their general direction. This was clearly going to be very messy indeed. Her weapon of choice was 'I Dreamed a Dream' from *Les Misérables*. It was, as Simon pointed out, a 'big song'.

Then she sang. It took only until the first line for the audience to cheer and for Ant and Dec to deliver a pair of perfectly executed turns to camera. 'Yerz didn't expect that, did you?' Ant demanded of us – the presenters had known what was coming. 'Did you? No!'

Like an epidemic, shock spread through the audience and they got to their feet and clapped as Susan Boyle sang. Simon Cowell smiled. The greatest of all his 'journeys' had begun.

THIRTEEN
THE GRINCH WHO STOLE CHRISTMAS

Simon Cowell later admitted that he felt ashamed when thinking about his initial, dismissive reaction to Susan Boyle when she walked on stage at the SECC. 'When I watched it back it was quite uncomfortable to watch,' he later told the BBC's *Newsnight* programme. 'But I was happy to admit I was wrong.'

Cowell's shame would become heightened when Susan Boyle's background became apparent. The youngest of four brothers and six sisters, she was starved of oxygen at birth. Susan was born – on April Fool's Day 1961 – with mild brain damage, which affected her ability to learn in later life. 'You're looking at someone who would get the belt every day: "Will you shut up, Susan!" – whack!' is how she later described her school days to the *Mirror*. 'I was often left behind at school because of one thing or another. I was a slow learner. I'm just I'm a wee bit slower at picking things up than other people. So you get left behind in a system that just wants to rush on, you know? That was what I felt was happening to me. There's nothing worse than another person having power over you by bullying you and you not knowing how to get rid of that thing.'

In a sense she never did get rid of that bullying: at the time of her audition she was known in the village where she lived as 'Susie Simple'. She was also referred to as 'Rambo' because of her ability to get very upset indeed if things didn't go her way. She lived on benefits and did voluntary work. Susan and her mum Bridget loved to watch TV talent shows, and it was her mum who encouraged her to enter *Britain's Got Talent*. Bridget Boyle never got to see her daughter's triumph though: she died in 2007. It was then that Susan Boyle was truly alone. 'After Mum died it didn't fully register until maybe six months after. That's when the loneliness set in and there was nobody around except my cat Pebbles. My confidence was pretty down at that time. A good way of levelling it out, I found, was to tell myself that even though she's not here physically, mentally and spiritually she is. That's what keeps you going. I have my faith, which is the backbone of who I am, really.'

Boyle's 'backstory' was no neat tale that could just be used to spin a yarn for PR purposes. She would have to be treated with great care by Cowell and his team during her time on the programme – it was likely that she would become fairly famous throughout Britain on the strength of her appearance on the stage of the SECC, particularly after the newspapers were tipped off about her performance to maximise publicity for the new series. But the producers weren't prepared for what happened next. The wave of appreciation for Boyle's performance that night was reproduced across the world via the internet after her audition was shown on television on 11 April. The video of her performance spread like a cyber-virus. By the time the following week's programme was on air, nearly 90 million people had viewed 'SuBo's' rendition of 'I Dreamed a Dream' online. She was in demand across the globe and began doing interviews with US news programmes. She even appeared on a live link to the Oprah Winfrey show. Boyle was interviewed by Winfrey on a link between Scotland and Chicago. Cowell – still dashing back and forth between *American Idol* and *Britain's Got Talent* – was in the US studio with Winfrey. The singer was by now sporting a slightly more polished appearance – she said all she had done was 'tidy myself up like any other female would have done'.

In fact Simon had enlisted some help in rebooting Boyle's appearance – she'd been nicknamed the 'Hairy Angel' by the press – but he didn't want her to be made over too quickly. He got the help of a makeup artist who was a regular on the set of *American Idol* – a striking Afghan-born brunette called Mezhgan Hussainy.

Hearing Boyle's story and seeing her frugal life in Blackburn, Winfrey asked her a painfully personal question: was she lonely? 'Oh, no. I am not lonely. Everyone has been so nice. I've got millions of new friends now.'

More than 17 million new friends tuned into the final of *Britain's Got Talent* on 30 May. Unfortunately, many of Susan Boyle's newfound admirers forgot to vote for her and the competition was won by an 11-piece street-dance collective called Diversity. The young dancers – led with chilling efficiency by choreographer Ashley Banjo – were clearly resigned to getting second place after the astonishing exposure that Boyle had received. 'To be honest, we thought we had no chance,' Banjo told journalists at a press conference following their win. 'We just went out there aiming to give the best performance we possibly could. So to come away as winners was amazing. We still haven't got used to it. Susan was so gracious about it. She was so nice about the whole thing, and behind the stage she was no different. She's just a really nice lady and I'm sure she'll do brilliantly.'

But, behind the scenes, the situation had in fact fallen in on Boyle. It's claimed she ranted and swore at production staff, threw water at one crew member and shouted, 'I hate this show. I hate it.' Her behaviour worsened to the extent that the police and an ambulance were called to her hotel in Westminster the following day and she was taken to the Priory recovery centre in Southgate, north London.

News leaked out quickly and ITV released a rather dry statement about Boyle's condition: 'Following Saturday night's show, Susan is exhausted and emotionally drained,' it said. 'She has been seen by her private GP who supports her decision to take a few days out for rest and recovery. We offer her our ongoing support and wish her a speedy recovery.'

Unusually, Professor Chris Thompson, chief medical officer of the Priory Group, spoke out on Boyle's apparent breakdown and voiced his concern over the pressures that had led her to this point: 'I would want to know that people being exposed to such pressures are actually looked after,' he told the *Daily Mail*. 'I think I know what TV companies would say – they would say, "These people are willing volunteers." The fact that there is consent between the TV company and contestant does not prevent the TV company having a duty of care once that consent has been given.'

'Duty of care' was the phrase that would crop up constantly when people discussed Susan Boyle's astonishing rise to fame. Had Simon caused harm to Boyle by allowing her to be on the show in the first place and by orchestrating the storm around her? 'I had total responsibility for the fact that we had auditioned her for the show, we put her through and we created this enormous press story,' he said. 'The week leading up to the finals, I didn't realise how much pressure she was under that week, with all the scrutiny. So I accept total, full responsibility for that'

Judge Piers Morgan – a particular favourite of Susan's – had his own take on what had happened. He told the *Daily Mail*: 'I do think it may turn out to be the best thing that happens to her, coming second. I think she has found a lot of it quite hard to deal with and I think the pressure of actually winning and living up to all that expectation would have just carried on the mayhem for her. I'm only sorry that the extraordinary tidal wave of publicity she attracted meant so many people got either bored or irritated by Boyle mania and decided not to vote for her.'

Even the Prime Minister got involved: 'I hope Susan

Boyle is OK,' Gordon Brown told the BBC, 'because she is a really, really nice person. I spoke to Simon Cowell last night – I wanted to be sure she was all right.'

Susan's brother Gerry explained the situation from the family's point of view to *Channel 4 News*. 'It's a huge show, it's a huge opportunity. She's been subjected to a huge media frenzy. But she put herself there, she knows what she's doing. She's enjoying it. She loves the attention, but unfortunately a few things over the weekend culminated in her getting a bit anxious and overworried.'

Another of Susan's brothers – John – was less diplomatic. In an interview with the *Edinburgh Evening News*, he said, 'She has been constantly hounded by fans for the past seven weeks. Like anyone, she has a breaking point – she is only human after all. Celebrities have professional people who insulate them from these stresses but she hasn't had this protection.'

Gerry Boyle added that it wasn't the fact that she had lost that had caused his sister so much distress. In her mind, the end of the series signalled the end of her dream and she would now simply return to her village and be forgotten about. 'Susan feels that as long as she has a career in show business, as long as she can sing, then it's all been worthwhile. Susan's personality is that she worries about things, she gets upset about things. Her main concern is, Where do I go from here? Do people want to hear me sing? Is there a career for me?'

When Susan was well enough, Cowell held a meeting with the singer and several members of her family. The issue of what would happen next was at the top of the agenda. 'One thing she asked me was, Will this go on for ever?' Cowell told the BBC's Kirsty Wark. 'I said, "You're unstoppable – this could go on for as long as you want." I said to them [Boyle's family], "The truth is, if this is too much for her or she doesn't want to do it, we'll rip the contract up. No one's going to be forced into doing anything. This had to be her decision – we're happy to do this but, if you think it's the wrong thing, we'll walk away." '

In June, despite more concerns for her and her no-show at some of the dates on the *Britain's Got Talent* tour, it was announced that Susan Boyle had signed to Simon's label Syco.

Details of another kind – even more lucrative than a Susan Boyle contract – were first hinted at during that summer too. And for the first time the words 'Cowell' and 'Billion' began appearing in newspaper headlines. The stories centred on a business link-up between Simon and his friend Sir Phillip Green. The retail tycoon – he owns Topshop and BHS – had palled up with Simon in the late 1990s and Green was another regular at Sandy Lane in Barbados. The rumoured deal between the two men was of global proportions: an entertainment empire controlling the rights and content to Simon's shows that could rival the reach and power of Disney. A key element would be taking *The X Factor* to the US. The pair's formidable mix of business styles was described by one 'insider' in the pages of the *Daily Mail* in terms that would worry anyone who would have to face them across a boardroom table: 'For the past few months Sir Philip has been sitting in on

Cowell's negotiations as his contracts with Sony and *American Idol* are up for renewal,' said the source. 'He's been acting like a manager. They have a bit of a good cop, bad cop routine ... with Cowell as the good cop. They are talking about making profits running into billions as opposed to millions.'

As the business world buzzed with rumours of the deal, Simon himself was straight into the audition process for the next *X Factor* series. Inspired by the live audience reactions to the *Britain's Got Talent* auditions, the same format was transferred to the *X Factor*. All four judges returned but the series will be remembered for three things that totally overshadowed the competition itself, the first being the campaign to keep the winning single off the Christmas Number 1 slot, the second being John, the third being Edward.

Seventeen-year-old twins John and Edward Grimes auditioned for the show in Glasgow with all guns blazing. Simon for one was confused by their American accents – they're well brought up boys from Dublin – as they bounded onto the stage with their skinny ties and vertical blond quiffs and vibed up the audience as if they were returning for an encore. When Cheryl Cole asked them where they saw themselves in 15 years' time, the answer she got was, 'Older.' To general bafflement they staggered their way through the Backstreet Boys' 'As Long as You Love Me.' Their performance was, at best, rubbish. There was a reason for this: 'That was our first, very first time singing on a microphone,' John later admitted to *Digital Spy*. 'We've improved a lot since then. We could go back over our performances and say that we could do better or change what we did, but you can't go back on anything you do.'

Despite the fact that Simon branded them 'not very good and incredibly annoying' from the word go, the twins would claim to have an affinity with the judge. 'We think he's like us,' they later told *Q* magazine. 'He went to a posh school – his story is the same as ours.'

When *X Factor* 6 went on air in August, it was clear that the series had a strong mix of characters and styles as well as the comedy element of the twins. There was every-bloke soul boy Olly Murs, hirsute pub rocker Jamie 'Afro' Archer, guileless single mum Stacey Solomon and South Shields teen Joe McElderry. But the headlines kept coming back to the twins, by now christened 'Jedward' with a crushing inevitability. 'The twins are deluded in such a funny way that they're genuinely not aware how bad they are,' Simon told Chris Tarrant during a radio interview. 'They just live in the twins' world. I haven't really had a proper conversation with them but people who have spoken to them say they're just not aware of anything. They think they're pop stars and everything's fantastic and they obviously hear something different to the rest of the world. I sit there thinking, "I've got to get over my personal feelings." I've got to find something positive or constructive to say at the end of this performance. And each week they get progressively worse and that's when I get frustrated.'

The trouble with the twins, though, was that because of the momentum of publicity they were building up – and despite their awful performances – there was a developing sense of danger that they could actually win the series. 'If you allow – which I think is right – the public to determine who wins, you've got to go with it,' Simon said. 'You don't have to agree with it but you have to go with it.'

In September, the public determined that they could not wait for Susan Boyle's debut album. *I Dreamed a Dream* went to Number 1 on the Amazon charts – three months before it was due for release. The astonishing level of pre-orders was a taste of things to come. It debuted at Number 1 on the US *Billboard* chart and in Britain it became the fastest-selling debut in UK chart history – beating the previous record set by Leona Lewis – and the biggest seller of 2009. The fact that the second-biggest seller would be the first album by JLS made things even sweeter for Simon.

Of course, winning – or indeed being runner-up – on one of Simon's shows was no guarantee of continuing success, as one of his former charges was about to find out. In September it was revealed that young dancer George Sampson had joined the long list of people dropped by Cowell. A spokeswoman for Syco put a positive spin on the situation: 'They could work together again in the future. The door is very much open for any other projects that come up.'

Sampson himself was somewhat less hopeful: 'Things aren't going so well with me and Simon. I suppose he's realised he can make more money out of other people.'

Young George may have fallen out with Simon, but Cowell did manage to rustle up 400 other friends to help celebrate his 50th birthday in October. The party was held in the Cowell heartland of Barnet, Hertfordshire, in the grounds of the Wrotham Park estate. It was a party of staggering excess and Cowell's face was everywhere: in a Michelangelo-style painting on the ceiling, on masks worn by waiters, in silhouette on the tablecloths and even projected 60 feet high onto the side of the Wrotham manor house itself.

There were baby sharks in the toilets, music from Il Divo, Westlife and Leona Lewis and a menu that reflected Simon's retro taste in grub: shepherd's pie, fish fingers and Alphabetti spaghetti soup that spelt out his name. Guests included Kate Moss, Naomi Campbell, Simon Fuller, Katie Price, fellow judges past and present including Louis Walsh, Dannii Minogue, Sharon Osbourne, Ryan Seacrest, Randy Jackson and Paula Abdul, TV chef Gordon Ramsay and – of course – Simon's mum Julie. Nicholas Cowell – always the best man for the job when it became to debunking Simon – made a speech about his brother's ex-girlfriends, including his last partner: 'They met on the internet and got really excited about each other. When they finally met, Simon was amazed to find that Terri can be a girl's name, too.'

Terri, of course, was there too. But among the guests was another woman who was becoming very close to Simon. Very close indeed. Tall and slim with long, dark hair and exotic, sculpted features that gave her a striking resemblance to Jackie St Clair, she wore a stunning, floor-length, white evening dress at the event and was photographed with Cowell, but the picture never made the newspapers over the following days. Snaps of sozzled stars leaving the bash in the early hours filled the press and provided a perfect smokescreen for the burgeoning romance between Simon and makeup artist Mezhgan Hussainy. A former model and soap opera actress – she had parts in *The Bold and the Beautiful* and *Sunset Beach* – she had been a long-time member of the *American Idol* team, doing Simon's makeup. And she had a backstory that made even some of Cowell's contestants look dull by comparison.

Born in 1973 into an upper-middle-class family in Afghanistan, in many ways she had an equivalent upbringing to Simon, with a nanny, a cook and a housekeeper helping her and her three brothers. Her mother Mary was a teacher, her father Sayed worked in IT and employed up to 40 people. Their life changed for ever with the Soviet invasion of Afghanistan. The family fled, fearing conscription for their sons into the army and the destructive power of Soviet bombers. They paid smugglers to help them make their escape – Mezhgan's mother had sewn money into her skirt to make sure they had enough to ensure their safety. 'It took us ten days on foot through the mountains and the Khyber Pass. We were tired and hungry,' she later recalled. 'Every day I thank my parents for taking the decision to leave Afghanistan when they did.'

The family finally it made it Pakistan, where they stayed for nine months before getting permission to move to the States – Mezhgan's father had been educated in the US. The striking-looking teenager got some modelling work and some walk-on parts in TV, something the family were wary of. 'At first I was confused and did not understand why my parents were advising me to be cautious of modelling and acting,' she later told *Zeba* magazine. 'This was something that I enjoyed doing and took great pleasure in. Pursuing a career in modelling and acting is possible for any Afghan girl, as long as she remains true to herself and her culture and does not portray herself in a manner that would force the community to look down upon her. Anything can be done right, with moderation and within limits.'

She also got jobs selling makeup at the Robinson-May department store in Los Angeles and enrolled on a dental-hygiene course (that might come in handy). She got TV work doing makeup for American game show host and actor John O'Hurley before joining *American Idol*, and meeting Cowell.

Rumours about the pair's romance began appearing in the press later in August. As ever, Max Clifford swung into action: 'Simon's friendship with her is purely platonic. They are not romantically involved.'

Meanwhile, it was Simon's business relationships that managed to grab the headlines away from his private life as more details emerged about his link-up with Sir Philip Green. In an interview with *GQ* magazine – under the headline SIMON COWELL AND HIS $1 BILLION DEAL OF THE CENTURY, it was revealed that *The X Factor* was indeed heading to America, with initial talk being of an internet-based deal, perhaps with a permanent *X Factor* production base in Las Vegas (this was later taken off the table). Green was also interviewed for the piece: 'It'll all be online,' he said. 'You have 20, 30, 40 million people tuning in twice a week. You bring two or three hundred million viewers to a venue. It's turning it up a peg.'

Cowell said that not taking the show to America – the biggest market in the world – would be crazy. It was hard to argue with his logic: the influential *Forbes* magazine had just named Simon the highest male earner on US television, with an estimated take-home pay of $75 million from 2008 to 2009. He was now looking at the show in the way that Grand Prix events had been developed into a global brand by Formula One boss Bernie Ecclestone. 'I like the model of what Bernie Ecclestone has done,' he said. 'The Singapore race is as good as the French race is as good as the English race.'

Simon certainly seemed to have found a kindred spirit in the shape of retail boss Green. 'In a funny way, we're in the same business,' Green said. 'We both understand the consumer – we know what the public wants.'

Cowell's dominance of the world entertainment market was nearly complete. But it left one question unanswered: what would happen to the gentlemen's agreement not to move *The X Factor* to the US while Simon was still doing *American Idol*?

While all this was going on, the British version of *The X Factor* was heading towards the final showdown and, fortunately for music lovers everywhere, John and Edward fell by the wayside after seven weeks of headline-grabbing madness. It left the competition down to a straight fight between Olly Murs, Stacy Solomon and Joe McElderry, with McElderry the eventual winner. The song Simon had chosen as the winner's single was 'The Climb', made famous by tween TV idol Miley Cyrus and featured in her recent *Hannah Montana* movie. It was a classic 'journey' song and all bets were off in terms of its being the Christmas Number 1 – it was a sure thing. That was until this message appeared on Facebook: 'Fed up of Simon Cowell's latest karaoke act being Christmas No 1? Me too . . . So who's up for a mass-purchase of the track "Killing in the Name" from 13th December (don't buy it yet!) as a protest to *The X Factor* monotony?'

The page was set up by Essex couple Jon and Tracy Morter and the song they chose was a 1992 track by the sweary American political rap metallers Rage Against The Machine. Not only was the song an expletive-ridden rant against doing what 'they' tell you to do, it was exactly the kind of fearsome din that Cowell had been turning his nose up at ever since he got his first whiff of punk in the 1970s. 'It's been taken on by thousands in the group as a defiance to Cowell's music machine,' Morter told the *New Musical Express*, which quickly got behind the campaign. 'Some certainly see it as a direct response to him personally.'

The *NME* felt so aggrieved about the situation it put Simon on its pre-Christmas front cover, under the headline THE GRINCH SPEAKS!.

To his credit, Cowell agreed to be interviewed and to field questions from readers and musicians such as Johnny Marr of the Smiths, Biffy Clyro vocalist Simon Neil and electro-pop singer La Roux, who nailed her colours to the mast fairly quickly by asking, 'How do you feel about ruining the music industry?'

'Well, look, that's her opinion,' Cowell countered.

'What La Roux has to understand is that the music industry isn't dominated by us, or influenced by us for that matter. It's influenced by people who buy records and I believe in democracy.'

Clearly thriving on the cut and thrust of the interview, Simon went even further, suggesting that the record-buying public – and the readers of the *NME* – actually owed him a debt of thanks. 'I think we were getting to a point where it was all becoming like [Cliff Richard's] "The Millennium Prayer". I just didn't like that song. I think we all have this belief that the Christmas Number 1 was just amazing songs. But actually when you look at them over recent years it was Bob the Builder, Mr Blobby … there's a tradition of quite horrible songs. I think I've done everyone a favour.'

As the battle lines were drawn, much was made of the fact that Rage Against the Machine were a Sony act, as was Joe McElderry. Many claimed this undermined the point of the campaign if the same company was going to benefit. 'Rage was a perfect choice, we couldn't give a toss what label it's on,' was Jon and Tracy's response. 'Get over it.'

It was the biggest pop-music battle since Blur were pitted against Oasis in the Britpop war of 1995. As with that great chart battle, you had to decide whose side you were on. Everyone had to have an opinion, especially those involved: 'If it had been an original song they would have had a point and it would have been fun and had something organic about it,' was *X Factor* presenter Dermot O'Leary's take when asked during an appearance on *The One Show*. 'Joe – a really lovely kid – versus a little band that's come from nowhere. The fact that it was a re-release and that they're both signed to Sony sullied it a bit for me.'

Cowell initially seemed more irked than worried: 'If there's a campaign – and I think the campaign's aimed directly at me – it's stupid,' he told reporters at an *X Factor* press conference that should have been about the final three contestants. 'My having a Number 1 record at Christmas is not going to change my life particularly,' Cowell said. 'I think it's quite a cynical campaign geared at me that is actually going to spoil the party for these three.'

When the three became one and *The X Factor* winner was announced as Joe McElderry, the South Shields teenager was thrust into the limelight. He was asked if he was gay (no), he was asked if he was a virgin (yes) and he was asked to give his opinion on the track that was vying with his song for the Christmas Number 1 slot (he wasn't too keen). 'They can't be serious!' he said after the *Sun* played him 'Killing in the Name'. 'I had no idea what it sounded like. It's dreadful and I hate it. How could anyone enjoy this? Can you imagine the grandmas hearing this over Christmas lunch? I wouldn't buy it. It's a nought out of ten from me. Simon Cowell wouldn't like it. They wouldn't get through to boot camp on *The X Factor* – they're just shouting. I think people are jumping on this to have a go at Simon and *The X Factor* rather than me. But Simon gives people a shot. I will be really disappointed if it doesn't go to number one after all the effort I've put into this and winning the show.'

When the chart placings were announced, Rage Against the Machine won the day selling 50,000 more than Joe.

'Make no mistake about it, this was a political act,' RATM's Tom Morello told the *NME*. 'This was an entire nation delivering a stinging slap of rejection to the whole notion of prefabricated pop ruling the charts. And Rage's victory over *The X Factor* was an act of God.'

Simon was a little more gracious in defeat – he contacted Jon and Tracy Morter to congratulate them. 'He was very nice, really nice to talk to,' Jon Morter told the *Mirror*. 'We had a little chat about music and just things in general really. He was lovely and he wished us well and he also said it was probably the best Christmas number one race that he has been involved with.'

'I am genuinely impressed by the campaign they've run,' Cowell said. 'It's been a good campaign with no dirty tricks and without any funding. They've been passionate and worked hard. I offered them jobs at my record company. I wanted them to come and work for me. I was deadly serious but they haven't taken me up on the offer.'

One offer Simon didn't take up was the option to renew his contract with *American Idol*. The ninth series, it was announced on 11 January 2010, would be his last, clearing the way for an American version of *The X Factor*. The deal went down to the wire – it's believed Simon was still on the phone thrashing out the final details as he drove to the press conference to announce it. He could have walked away if his terms weren't met. They were.

Harking back to the court cases between Cowell and Simon Fuller when *The X Factor* was launched in Britain, journalists began rubbing their hands again at the prospect of a Simon-versus-Simon battle fought on American soil.

Fuller seemed sniffy with regard to the content of *The X Factor*. The knowing comparison he made was that *The X Factor* was like wrestling compared with the purer, more sporting challenge of *Idol*, which he likened to boxing. This was surely a dig at Cowell with his past connections to the noble entertainment of wrestling. 'I want *Idol* to be purely about talent,' Fuller told *The Times*. 'We're not going to be led into the mud, we're going to stay on our hill.' Fuller maintained that *Idol* would be about singers like Kelly Clarkson rather than the 'Susan Boyle phenomenon, which is not based on anything but the bizarre'. Fuller was adamant: if this meant fewer viewers then so be it.

Speculation went into overdrive over whether *Idol* could survive without Simon – and, if it could, who should replace him. Names were being thrown around like confetti – everyone from shock jock Howard Stern to gossip blogger Perez Hilton to Oasis guitarist Noel Gallagher was being mentioned in connection with the job. One recurring name was that of Elton John. He could deliver a putdown with the best of them, but in the past the singer had been critical of Simon's shows. '*The X Factor* is a cruise ship show. I've got nothing against the people who go on – good luck to them – but I hate how they're treated,' John told the *Mirror*. 'They're given an awful sense of stardom and pressure straightaway but they're only successful until the next series. The record companies sell a lot of records and those people are gone. It's fucking cruel.'

There was of course one person who was ideally placed to advise the makers of *American Idol* on whom they should recruit: Simon Cowell. 'You just have to find somebody who can actually make a difference to the contestants, who's not afraid to speak their mind, who's prepared to be honest and occasionally blunt, but not to be gratuitously rude – I'm really getting tired of all of that now,' Simon said when reporters in America asked his opinion. 'But look, there'll be a lot of people, as you know, who want the job. I think, ironically, it's going to help next season because I think there's going to be a lot of interest as to who replaces me.'

Simon's quitting would leave Randy Jackson as the only remaining judge from the original line-up. The big man took Cowell's departure hard. 'Listen, he's my best friend … one of my best friends in the world. The guy is über-smart. He looks at the whole picture. He looks at life on the show in a way no one else looks [at it]. I love him. I'm just gonna miss sitting next to him, learning from him. I don't think you can replace him. I think you move with somebody different in that seat. It's a tough thing. We've been talking about it. We'll see where we end up.'

Those who knew Cowell best could see the bigger picture. The new deal was the thing he'd be striving for, the culmination of nearly ten years of planning. Some believed that this was his long-term goal when he first agreed to do *Pop Idol* all those years ago. 'He wants to own everything,' Pete Waterman told CNN. 'He wants to be the biggest, he wants to be a billion-dollars-a-year man and he's going to be the first guy to do that. It's not about the money for him. He wants to say that he created history by being the first man that became a worldwide brand. He doesn't own

American Idol and he only gets paid to appear on the show, but he does own *X Factor* and he owns the whole brand. Simon believed that he could dominate television and I've got to be honest, but that is an incredible assumption that I'd never seen anyone make. If you told me that Cowell would now be the biggest entertainer on the planet – we're talking about someone who doesn't present, who doesn't sing, who doesn't dance – he does one thing. And that's being Simon Cowell.'

FOURTEEN
TRUTHFULLY, GENUINELY, HONESTLY

'It doesn't matter if you like it or not,' Radio 1 DJ Chris Moyles told his listeners after he played Simon's single for the victims of the Haiti earthquake at just after eight in the morning on 2 February 2010, 'It's what it's all *about*.'

What it was about was an attempt to help the families of the 200,000 victims of the massive quake, which struck on Tuesday, 12 January. The project that Simon had announced backstage at the National Television Awards a few days after the disaster was now a reality – a Band Aid for a new generation. Despite the good intentions, Moyles for one felt the list of acts featured on the song – a cover of REM's 'Everybody Hurts' – was 'random'. They included Leona Lewis, Take That, Jon Bon Jovi, Susan Boyle, Robbie Williams, Miley Cyrus and Rod Stewart. Most had either made it thanks to Simon or appeared as guests on his shows. The choice of song was a straightforward one guided by the sentiment of the lyrics, rather than an indication that Simon was a major fan of REM, the kind of left-field act loved by rock critics and therefore not really on his radar. In an interview with the *Sun*, REM's manager, Bertis Downs, confirmed that the band would be waiving all royalties for 'Everybody Hurts'. 'We are deeply touched the song has been chosen for this Haiti campaign,' Downs said. 'It means a lot that the song the guys wrote all those years ago will be used for such an important appeal.'

Prime Minister Gordon Brown said in January, 'The agony and anguish for the people that we are seeing on our television screens is something that British people want to respond to. Simon Cowell can make a huge amount of money to help the people of Haiti.'

Unsurprisingly, 'Everybody Hurts' went to Number 1 on Valentine's Day, selling half a million copies in the first week of release. Other artists did what they could to help: Rihanna released a cover version of Bob Marley's classic 'Redemption Song'; American stars such as Pink, Black Eyed Peas and Usher got involved in a rerecorded version of 'We Are the World', the eighties African famine relief song; even Simon's old enemies the punks got involved, with former members of the Sex Pistols, The Clash, Shane MacGowan of The Pogues, The Pretenders' Chrissie Hynde and actor Johnny Depp recording 'I Put a Spell on You', the 1956 Screamin' Jay Hawkins song.

MacGowan told the *Guardian* he put the song together as a direct response to Cowell's release: 'When I heard that shite I thought, fuck it, let's show him how it's done … and that's how we came to do our version of "I Put a Spell on You". That's what a charity single should sound like.'

In the United States, Simon's final outing as an *American Idol* judge was under way. There was no Paula Abdul this time. She'd announced on Twitter her decision to quit: 'With sadness in my heart, I've decided not to return to *Idol*,' she wrote. 'I'll miss nurturing all the new talent, but most of all being a part of a show that I helped from day one become an international phenomenon.'

Her contract had run out at the end of the last season and there was talk of her making demands for a major pay rise. It was claimed that Abdul had gone into rehab in California after a series of injuries and accidents left her with a serious painkiller habit. She claimed the medication disrupted her sleep patterns and made her act 'weird'. 'I could have killed myself,' Abdul told *Ladies' Home Journal*, not usually a place to find showbiz rehab confessions. 'Withdrawal – it's the worst thing. I was freezing cold, then sweating hot, then chattering and in so much pain. It was excruciating. But at my very core, I did not like existing the way I had been.'

She then denied the claims. 'It was very stressful for me to hear that and to be quoted saying something I've never said … I've never checked into a rehab clinic. I've never been addicted or abused drugs, and I've never been addicted or abused alcohol. I've never even been drunk in my life,' she told Detroit radio show *Mojo in the Morning*. The journalist had got it all wrong:'It's a *spa*. I was there for almost three days having fun doing spa stuff. It's not a clinic. It's not a detox place. It's a luxurious spa. It's like taking a mini vacation. I just wanted to chill out and get massages and maybe a manicure and pedicure.' The *Ladies' Home Journal* stood by its story.

Abdul may have come across a touch batty at times, but her enthusiasm and apparent lack of cynicism had acted as a vital counterpoint to Cowell's far more sour persona – she was the good cop to his bad cop. The final series of *American Idol* just wouldn't be the same without her. 'I miss Paula – she was great fun,' Simon told the US chat-show host Jay Leno. 'It's a different show without her. I will definitely be doing something with her.'

Paula's eventual replacement was comedienne and talk-show host Ellen DeGeneres, an unlikely choice for the format. Cowell had given plenty of interviews saying that his replacement needed to have an industry background – so why was DeGeneres on board? 'The reason Ellen was a good choice is because she actually is very responsible for people she has performing on her own show. I know that for a fact because I've dealt with her as a record label, and she loves music and she's been an artist. It wasn't meant to dis her credentials: it was specifically talking about my replacement because my role on the show was somebody who has run a successful record label.'

As the auditions got under way, it was clear that there were plenty of people left in America with slightly distorted opinions of their own abilities. In Orlando, Florida, super-confident contestant Jarrod Norrell delivered a nails-scraped-across-a-blackboard version of 'Amazing Grace'. When he was told he sounded like a lawnmower he just kept on singing and singing – until he was led out by security guards. Simon Cowell – with a comedy timing that had been honed to perfection over the previous eight series – turned to his fellow judges and calmly asked, 'Yes or no?'

In Atlanta, 62-year-old 'General' Larry Platt went directly from contestant to internet sensation in one mighty leap with his rendition of his own composition, the insanely catchy 'Pants on the Ground'. The song, a firm rebuke to those who don't pull their trousers up properly, clearly struck a chord with Simon Cowell: 'I have a horrible feeling that song could be a hit.' Platt found himself with a million fans on Facebook and on the lips of every comedian in America.

Back in Britain, Simon's schedule meant he had to jet over to film auditions for *Britain's Got Talent*. Mezhgan Hussainy accompanied him to the London leg of the filming and the paparazzi got their first shots of the pair together, despite some elaborate entrances and exits from some of Simon's favourite restaurants. The party line from Simon's spokesman was that the pair were just friends. This didn't stop bookmakers William Hill offering 4–1 that the couple were about to announce their engagement.

With speculation mounting, Cowell took control of the situation. He recorded an interview for Piers Morgan's *Life Stories* show for ITV. In it they talked about Simon's childhood, his fall from grace in the eighties, his success and his relationships. Cowell chose this safe environment – Morgan is effectively an employee – to come clean about his relationship with Mezhgan. 'I am smitten with Mezhgan. I think she's the one.'

In front of a studio audience – with Mezhgan among them – Simon even discussed the previously unthinkable: having children. 'I think I possibly need to have a few more

Simons around. The thing about kids it's something you have to believe you're in for the long term – 100 per cent.'

But, despite the seriousness of the topic and his tone, Simon couldn't resist sending the moment up slightly by slipping in a joke: 'You just know when you've found someone special and I feel very, very happy – for her.'

Someone else who was very happy was Simon's mum, Julie. Simon rang her, warning her that he had something important to tell her. 'He explained to me that he had asked Mezhgan to move in with him,' she told *Hello!*. 'Although girlfriends had stayed with him in the past, he had never done that before. This seemed to make it official. What baffled me most is the complete turnaround in my son. He has always insisted, "I'm fine as I am, Mother. I'm not going to get committed to a marriage and I certainly don't want children." I used to reply, "You don't know, you've never had them." I really think marriage and fatherhood is going to happen for Simon.'

While the Piers Morgan interview was relatively within Cowell's comfort zone, the next appearance he made with Mezhgan very clearly wasn't. Crossing the Atlantic he appeared on Jay Leno's *Tonight* show, ostensibly to promote his final season of *American Idol*. Initially, Simon went into his default flippant mode: 'I do have somebody in my life now. I kind of made a decision this year to make somebody happy. It's called giving back.'

But Leno went in hard, pushing Simon on whether he was in fact engaged, if he'd bought a ring – he had, in London – and then dragged Mezhgan out from the wings to sit briefly with Simon and exchange a deeply uncomfortable kiss with him. 'I'm blushing,' Cowell told the chat-show host, somewhat unnecessarily.

When photos appeared of Mezhgan wearing a hefty-looking ring, Terri Seymour was the first to congratulate the pair. 'I'm so happy for him – I'm delighted for them both,' she told the *Mirror*. 'It's great to see Simon so happy. There's absolutely no awkwardness between me and him. He's like my best mate. I'm hoping I can come to the wedding but it will all depend on work.'

Privately, it's believed Seymour wrote to Mezhgan to offer her congratulations woman to woman: 'You've accomplished the impossible … making Simon happy.'

On 17 April the *Britain's Got Talent* circus came into town again as the show came back on air. Simon made a point of managing people's expectations of the new series. Viewers shouldn't expect another Susan Boyle, he warned. He also admitted that the SuBo factor had fundamentally changed the way he now approached the programme and the contestants. 'Because of what happened last year with Susan, we are aware of what can happen to people,' he told journalists at the launch of the new series. 'So 12 months later you approach it in a very, very different way and you are aware that pressure can do all sorts of things to people. You are hyper-, hyper-aware of any audition you do. You have to feel they can cope with what's coming if you put them through. They are under massive, massive scrutiny now and it's one of those things. I'm glad I gave Susan the opportunity. I wouldn't change that because we're helping her live her dreams; we're giving her a shot.'

The show got under way with the usual menagerie of naked balloon dancers, tambourine bashers, musical burpers and mashed-potato-eating parrots. An early standout was 10-year-old Chloe Hickinbottom, a guaranteed crowd-pleaser who sang a moving rendition of 'The White Cliffs of Dover', made famous by forces sweetheart Vera Lynn. Simon missed her performance after being laid low by flu, but Piers Morgan was there to make sure she went through: 'It's hard to imagine a better act for the Royal Variety Performance,' he said.

When Simon was ill, his place was taken by Louis Walsh. The Irishman looked odd sitting next to Piers Morgan and Amanda Holden, and seemed more interested in playing with the buzzers that the judges use to get rid of the acts than the acts themselves. But it did prompt the question: could *Britain's Got Talent* run without Cowell? Simon admitted that the show was becoming too much for him. It was the first sign that perhaps his American ambitions may soon start to take priority. 'I am looking at *BGT* and whether I have a different role, maybe coming in at a later stage. I like the show but it takes a hell of a lot of time. You sit there watching horrific acts and you think, I genuinely can't do this any more. I'm considering, next year, coming in for the semi-finals, just the studio bit. Can I see the show without me? Yes, it can work without me. But you have to really know what you are talking about – you have to be able to spot a star, nurture them, mentor them.'

May 2010 saw Simon's last appearance as a judge on *American Idol*. Cowell's departure – and talk of who would replace him – had totally overshadowed the series which failed to capture the imagination of critics or public. The finale was a chance for Cowell to bow out in style. Former winners and notable contestants returned to give Simon a big send-off and ex-judge Paula Abdul came back to make a rather cringe-making speech. When the time came for Simon to say his farewell, viewers were surprised to see him struggling to speak.

'I didn't think I was going to be this emotional,' he said, 'but I genuinely am.' Talking directly to the audience he added, 'The show goes forward. It'll be different. But you know what the truth is? When everyone asks who will replace me, who's going to be the next judge, the truth is you guys are the judge of this show. And you've done an incredible job over the years. It's been a blast.'

Almost as an afterthought it was announced that singing paint salesman Lee DeWyze had won the series, beating altogether more interesting hippy chick blues singer Crystal Bowersox into second place. DeWyze's victory song was 'Beautiful Day', the same U2 number sung by *World Idol* winner Kurt Nilsen some eight years earlier. The viewing figures for the final were the lowest since the first series but while the show's producers insisted Cowell's departure wasn't the end of *American Idol*, it certainly looked and felt like it.

For Simon, there was precious little time to dwell on the end of the *American Idol* era – he was back on a plane to judge the final stages of *Britan's Got Talent*. After the previous year's SuBo moment, the series was never likely to scale the same heights, but some of the acts served up had no business being on primetime television at all. Cross-dressing 'singers', a wood-chopper and a seemingly endless parade of dance acts battled it out with a singing great-granny, a teenage drummer and a barely-pubescent boy band. In the end it was the chillingly well-prepared gymnastic act Spelbound – that's the way they spell it – who won the day. Simon said their performances were 'like watching a master race', but there was not enough pure talent elsewhere in the show.

It was soon being suggested that the search for stars be broadened with a global version of the show, called *World's Got Talent*. Max Clifford was briefing the press about the idea as Spelbound were tumbling their way to victory. 'Simon knows that Susan Boyle is something that happens once in a blue moon,' Clifford said. 'Perhaps the current series will not produce a world star but it has given the contestants an enormous platform for their talent. *World's Got Talent* is one of a number of ideas being discussed but Simon has not made any firm decision yet.'

Firm decisions were in short supply in Simon's private life too. Speculation had mounted throughout 2010 about when he and Mezhgan would tie the knot. Interest peaked amid claims that the couple were planning four ceremonies in different parts of the world to accommodate the international nature of their guest list. Half-brother Tony Cowell had fanned the flames by announcing on his radio show: 'My mum is in Los Angeles sorting out the lovebirds and coming back, hopefully, with a wedding date. Mum's final words to me before she flew off to LA were, "Last year he said he was never, never, never going to get married and this year he's getting married four times; once in

Brighton, once in Los Angeles, once in Barbados on a yacht and once in Hollywood."'

Simon himself stepped forward to end the speculation: 'In spite of various people claiming to be making arrangements for our wedding, no such plans exist,' he said. 'When Mezhgan and myself decide the time is right, we will make our own plans. I just want to clarify the situation because I keep reading about different people planning our wedding.'

'He won't be getting married this year and he doesn't need to rush into it anyway,' close friend Nigel Lythgoe told the *News of the World*. 'Simon has a lot to do. He has to prepare himself for the American *X Factor* to try to create the next biggest show there and he'll be fully focused. Maybe he's just gearing himself up.'

There were even those who wondered whether it would ever happen. 'I really don't know if he will go through with it,' Sinitta told the *Mirror*. ' If he is really true to himself, he probably won't. He always said he never wanted to get married. He surprised us all.'

Of course, not everyone loves Simon quite as much as Mezhgan Hussainy does. Because of the power he wields, the influence he exerts, the money he generates and the way his tastes dictate so much of our popular culture, some people really don't like him. At all.

Chris Martin of Coldplay: 'He should be melted down and turned into glue.'

Former Oasis guitarist Noel Gallagher: 'People from Bradford singing in American accents? It's shite. It's really who's got the biggest sob story. It's all "Oh my cat died and its outstretched paw was pointing at a big X, so today, Simon, I'm going to sing 'What's New Pussycat?'." Do us a favour: get us a proper job. Simon Cowell says to the contestants that it's all about them. No, it's not: it's about you, Simon.'

Singer Phil Collins: 'I've got no time for Simon Cowell. I really think the show's all about being rude to people. Simon Cowell is just cruel and that's all there is to it. I saw one girl who sang on boats for a job and Simon said, "I'd never go on a boat you were singing on because it would sink." It's all about him being witty and cutting. That's what happens when they become more important than the people they're trying to help: you end up with a bunch of smart-asses. I really hate it.'

Even those who've worked with him and prospered because of him are not averse to criticising Simon Cowell. Robson Green: 'I think it's sad he's continued to do what he's doing because he's better than that. I don't mean that in a patronising way. He can do other things, great things, but, with his need to be a judge, he's become a one-trick pony.'

He has his supporters, too. Cheryl Cole: 'A lot of people think Simon is harsh and nasty but he's not, not one bit. He's got a heart of gold. He's really very charismatic and he's a pleasure to work with. He's always got time for people. He gets Northerners. The Northern mentality. I find a lot of people down South, if they've been brought up in quite a privileged way – public school or whatever – they're quite removed from what I am because I'm from a council estate in Newcastle, went to the most normal school, and that's worlds away from Simon. And yet he gets me, gets my humour.'

So in tune were Cowell and Cole that Simon's mum Julie even thought that at one stage that they might become a couple. 'Cheryl is a lovely girl – so beautiful,' Julie Cowell told *Hello!* magazine in 2010. 'I did wonder once wonder if Simon and Cheryl might have got together when Terri wasn't around. But no, they work too closely together and that's not healthy.'

With his megawatt smile and privileged life, it would be easy to assume that Cowell's life is perfect. He admits, though, that he has his dark side. He is clearly a workaholic. 'I am totally and utterly consumed by my work, almost to the point of obsession,' he told Piers Morgan in 2010. 'Almost every night I will be working till three, four, five in the morning. My life is kinda controlled by that.'

With business interests on both sides of the Atlantic, the office is virtually always open. And even a man with Cowell's ability to multi-skill can sometimes find things getting too much for him. 'I get to a point sometimes where I get overloaded, where you get a week or a month where you're responsible for so many things, where you have to deal with so many people – and this can go from leaving the office, till five or six in the morning if we have to deal with America – you've just had enough. Too much information. And at that point I will go on my own somewhere and work it out in my head. Without making it sound too dramatic, I deal with things myself. Sometimes you're happy sometimes you get a bit down …

when I'm down I like to be quiet. Sometimes you feel there's like a tidal wave of stuff that continues to come. You feel trapped.'

His answer to these feelings seems to be that, the day it genuinely becomes too much, he will walk away. In the meantime, Cowell has been nothing but open about who he is and what his intentions are. Look through every interview he's ever given and key words crop up all the time: *truthfully*, *genuinely*, *honestly*. These are his touchstones. You might not like what he's doing or the way that he's doing it, but at least he's giving it to you straight.

Speaking of which, has any British celebrity had his sexuality questioned more often and more rigorously than Simon Cowell? Perhaps because he is so blunt with others, journalists seem to think they can ask questions of him they wouldn't dare ask of any other A-lister. It's rare to find an interview with him or someone close to him where the issue doesn't come up: Simon, are you gay? 'I'm quite camp so I understand why people think that,' he told the *Daily Mail*, the newspaper that is interested in Cowell more than any other. 'I've always found it amusing because why would it be a problem if I were? I'm not in the Army. I work in an industry where there are a lot of gay people so I'd still sell records, I'd still be on television.'

But it doesn't end there: they want to know about his teeth (removable veneers), his hair (he's adamant he doesn't dye it), his fitness regime (press-ups and plenty of them) and whether he's had Botox: 'Yes I've had Botox,' he told the *Daily Mail*, 'but not in an obsessive way. Then again, every guy I know who works in the City has had it now. I am vain but, to be honest with you, I can't think of one person who's on TV who isn't vain. It's the nature of the beast. If you are on TV then you have a vanity, for sure. Just admit it!'

He's denied he's had plastic surgery, but Sinitta made a telling remark when she was asked by *New!* magazine in 2010 if she would consider going under the knife: 'Oh yeah I'm not anti it. Simon's work looks amazing and actually being able to see a friend up close makes me think, Well he looks good so if I ever do it, so will I.'

Perhaps it's a vital part of his appeal that, despite being just about the most famous person on earth, he's still 'one of us'. He's proud that he has the 'common touch' – in many ways it's the secret of his success. 'If you looked in my collection of DVDs, you'd see *Jaws* and *Star Wars,*' he says. 'In the book library you'd see John Grisham and Sidney Sheldon. And, if you look in my fridge, it's like children's food: chips, milkshakes, yoghurt. I don't have sophisticated tastes. I have average tastes.'

What he doesn't have, though, is average abilities. The music industry, we are constantly and confidently told, is dying. Technological file-sharing advances have made it increasingly difficult to make money from music. Yet one man has bucked the trend and made it more profitable than ever. Simon Cowell has fundamentally changed the way we access music and the kind of music we can expect to access. The model he dreamed up at the start of the 1990s to make sure he kept his job – using television to reach out directly to listeners rather than doing it via critics or radio playlists – has become the norm. It's changed the face of music and of television and been widely copied. The phenomenal success of the American TV show *Glee* and the way its tracks are made available straight after a show has been broadcast is a direct result of Simon Cowell.

He's a real product of the eighties – for him, greed is most definitely good and, despite his wealth and success, he retains the fierce streak of competitiveness that got him there in the first place. 'Simon always says to me whenever he makes a deal he gets three copies,' *American Idol* host Ryan Seacrest recently revealed to CNN. 'One copy for the attorney, one copy for himself and one copy to fax to me – so I weep.'

It's hard to criticise him for being obsessed by money, because he's so upfront about it: 'I'm interested only in making money, for myself and the people I work for,' he once told *Playboy* magazine. 'I mean, that's absolutely the only criteria I attach. That's it. That's the only thing we think about: Will it make money? And not just for us – for the artists as well. Let me tell you, artists are as interested in making money as we are. They're not donating their money to charity, trust me.'

As it happens, donating to charity is something that Cowell has done more than his fair share of. He's just been a little more discreet about it than most. There have been high-profile gestures: in 2008 he paid off the $162,000 mortgage of an American couple to ease their financial worries after their three-year-old daughter was diagnosed with cancer. He appeared on Oprah Winfrey's chat show with *X Factor* winner Leona Lewis to tell Amy and Randy Stoen from Minnesota that he would be their daughter

Madelaine's 'guardian angel'. 'I didn't know what to do in this situation other than to do something which I hope will help your situation. I know you're having problems with your mortgage. As of this afternoon, your mortgage has been paid off,' Cowell told a tearful Amy. Cowell later admitted, 'I never knew doing good could feel so good.'

In America, *Idol Gives Back* has become part of the TV calendar. A telethon-style event that has attracted guests from President Barrack Obama to Bono, it has raised more than $140 million for good causes. Cowell, who has visited Africa to see how *Idol Gives Back* money has been spent, saw the possibilities in mobilising the vast army of fans the show has created. If they were willing to vote then it was likely they were also willing to give. But he's also been adamant that the show itself must be entertaining, not just worthy. 'I think our main thing is to make sure that for anybody who's a fan of *American Idol*, is that they don't feel too uncomfortable and most importantly they enjoy the event as an entertainment show,' he told the *Los Angeles Times*. 'That is the number-one priority because, if we fail on that, this has all been a waste of time.'

In Britain, this side of Cowell has been more low-key. He's quietly lent his time and influence to the cause of children's hospices. Max Clifford: 'He probably won't thank me for saying it but in the years since we first met up, Simon's done an awful lot of things for an awful lot of people that no one knows anything about. The Chase [in Guildford] is a wonderful children's hospice where everything is done to make things as good as possible for as long as possible. Every single time *The X Factor* goes on air, there's children from that hospice and hospices all over the country who go to every show. They're Simon's guests and they go backstage and they meet Simon and he introduces them to everyone else and he makes a real fuss of them. More than that he's become an uncle to a lot of the kids. It's to his eternal credit.'

He has also donated his fame to the cause of fighting animal cruelty, appearing in adverts for the animal-rights organisation PETA – People for the Ethical Treatment of Animals. For any cause, there's great benefit to be had from someone so famous getting involved: it's an eye-catching gimmick to have someone so apparently uncaring asking us to care. It's also claimed that, while on holiday in Barbados in 2004, he gave a cheque for £10,000 to an animal shelter there after seeing the work it did – and made no mention of it. In the past Simon has said – maybe not entirely in jest – that he plans to leave all his money to animal charities in his will. With talk of his getting married and starting a family, that claim may well have to be adjusted.

He's recently been backing the WSPA (World Society for the Protection of Animals) campaign entitled 'Animals Matter To Me'. 'When I was growing up we had pets and I got – at an early age – to understand that you have to respect animals,' he stated in an interview for the WSPA website. 'I think where we are in the world today, I think animals deserve more protection. I don't understand how anyone can get pleasure from hunting or killing animals. I totally do not understand it. I think we've gone beyond that, I think there should be more international laws. The only way you can influence governments is by showing that you care. And if you care and tell someone else about it, then you start to create a movement. If you keep quiet about it, governments ignore you.'

Now there's a thought: Cowell the politician. Imagine what he could achieve if he put his skills and influence to effect on a bigger scale. He's actively thinking about how he could put the techniques he's perfected – instantly gauging the public's reaction to a person or performance – into wider use. Maybe even with politics. 'Now there are so many really, really, really hot topics,' he explained to *Newsnight*. 'For example, should we or shouldn't we be in Iraq or Afghanistan? If you asked most people in the country why are we there … I don't know why we're there. I knew why we were in the Falklands, I don't know why we're over there. When I see all these people coming back dead … I think we have a right to have a say in something like that.'

The key question for now though is, can he truly become his own man in America? He's broken free of *American Idol* – the concept owned by Simon Fuller – to potentially become the billion-dollar man, calling the shots with his own *X Factor* format. This time it really will be Simon versus Simon. 'Effectively Cowell and Fuller are going head to head for the same market,' Pete Waterman recently told *The Times*. 'There has to be a winner and there has to be a loser. There have been some defining moments in every era but this is the first time where there has been a clash of two different characters that will shape TV entertainment for the next five years. Cowell is banking on it [*American Idol*] not surviving. And Fuller's got a problem. He owns one of the greatest formats on Earth and suddenly he's potentially lost it. He's keeping the programme but he ain't keeping Simon Cowell.'

The business of being Simon Cowell is one that he clearly, unashamedly enjoys. He is a very good advert for the job of being very well known indeed. Unlike many people who are famous, Simon Cowell wears it well. Good thing, too, since he is now just about the most famous man in the planet. And he loves it: 'It's fantastic. Honest to God. I have had zero problems being well known, but not exactly a celebrity. Couldn't care less if someone wants to take my picture. Anyone who complains about invasion of privacy shouldn't work in the entertainment business. You can't have it both ways. It's as simple as that. I think there are too many people at the moment bleating about having a picture taken. Trust me. When the picture taking stops, they're going to be more unhappy. That's the way it is.'

No one loves a 'journey' more than Simon Cowell – and his has been like no other. The little boy who saw another world over the fence of his home in Barnet now has everything he wished for. Like all good journeys, it's changed the person who's taken it: 'I've definitely become more spoilt,' says the man who changed the world. 'Definitely become more shallow. And I can honestly say I have loved every single minute of it. It's the best job in the world.'

OUTRO
THE CAST

Simon Cowell may have changed the world, but he couldn't have done it all by himself. Here are the key people who came along for the ride and where they are now.

Paula Abdul: Things have been quiet for singer and choreographer since she left *American Idol*. It's claimed she's being considered as a judge for the forthcoming US version of *The X Factor*.

Kris Allen: The eighth winner of *American Idol* wasn't a favourite of Simon Cowell's, but Allen still returned to mentor new singers on the final series.

Ant and Dec: The duo who came into their own on the first series of *Pop Idol* now dominate ITV's entertainment schedules. Their new series *Push the Button* started in February 2010. The first episode featured a giant Simon Cowell head with dancing teeth.

Fantasia Barrino: The third winner of *American Idol* later revealed she had difficulties reading. She has since appeared in her own reality TV show called *Fantasia for Real*.

Steve Brookstein: The first *X Factor* winner is still singing; the press regularly like to chart his apparent fall from grace. In 2010 it was revealed he played to an audience of 50 at a pub in Cornwall.

Susan Boyle: The West Lothian singer is now a global star, but still struggles with stopping herself from calling Simon 'Mr Cowell'.

Kelly Brook: The short-lived judge for *Britain's Got Talent* recently appeared in the stage show *Calendar Girls* and the film *Piranha 3D*.

Alexandra Burke: In 2010 it was reported that *The X Factor* winner was being outsold by JLS at the rate of two to one. She told *Digital Spy*, 'I don't feel threatened by anything, because I think as long as you're working hard in this industry, good will come back to you.'

Nicki Chapman: The former *Pop Idol* judge is married to Dave Shackleton, vice president of Sony BMG records.

Kelly Clarkson: The first ever *American Idol* is still a major recording artist. In 2009 she had her first UK number one with the punky single 'My Life Would Suck Without You'.

Max Clifford: Simon's mum has a dog called Max named after Simon's spokesman. It's a terrier.

Cheryl Cole: The Girls Aloud singer, solo star and *X Factor* judge is now a Grade I listed national treasure.

John Cowell: Simon's half-brother runs Cowell Consulting, a construction consultancy, and is open about cashing in on the family name: 'I think of it as an asset if people are interested in meeting the relative of an A-list celebrity. If it gives me business, why be coy about it?'

Julie Cowell: The indomitable head of the Cowell clan lives near Brighton.

June Cowell: Simon's half-sister moved to Spain in her early 20s; she now lives in Majorca.

Michael Cowell: Simon's half-brother now uses the name Michael Bailey. Lost touch with Simon in the mid-1990s. He was the only family member who didn't appear on Simon's *This Is Your Life* show.

Nicholas Cowell: Simon's property-developer brother got his own reality show called *The Block* – it was not a success. The *Sun* said, '*The Block* can only refer to the mental one ITV had when it commissioned the programme.'

Tony Cowell: Writer Tony got his own TV show in the noughties called *Between the Covers*. 'Everything he has, I taught him,' he says of half-brother Simon. 'I'm not nasty, but I'm funnier than he is.'

Darius Danesh: The *Pop Idol* runner-up performed his Number 1 single 'Colourblind' on *Top of the Pops* with 'Underdog' written across the back of his jacket. Now calls himself Darius Campbell – star of stage and reality TV shows like *Popstar to Operastar*.

Diversity: The dance troupe beat Susan Boyle to win *Britain's Got Talent*. Leader Ashley Banjo has since tried his hand at reality-show judging on Sky's *Got to Dance*.

Five: The boy band split in 2001 only to re-form as a four-piece in 2006, predicting they would sell even more records the second time around. They didn't. Split up again six months later.

Jerome Flynn: The former *Soldier Soldier* star is now the voice of Daniel the Dog on the BBC kids' TV series *Tommy Zoom*.

Neil 'Dr' Fox: The *Pop Idol* judge received a lifetime achievement Sony award for services to radio in 2009. Contrary to popular belief, he is neither a real doctor nor a real fox.

Simon Fuller: The man who owns the *Idol* format has recently launched an online reality show called *If I Can Dream*, about a house full of showbiz wannabes in Hollywood.

Gareth Gates: The first *Pop Idol* runner-up is now a successful stage performer. 'I don't really speak to Simon any more. You know, I've moved on, we've all gone our separate ways, which is cool. It's all worked out for the best.'

Sir Philip Green: The billionaire retailer is now heavily involved in Cowell's expansion into the American market. He's also believed to have been the first choice to be the one to fire people from the BBC show *The Apprentice*.

Robson Green: The actor and sometime singer is still a mainstay of ITV's schedules and recently filmed a documentary about extreme swimming.

Justin Guarini: The first *American Idol* runner-up was dropped by the record label RCA after six months. He's since recorded jazz albums, worked as a TV presenter and acted in indie films.

David Hasselhoff: The man some people refer to only as the Hoff continues to be David Hasselhoff for a living. In 2010 he became a guest host for wrestling show *WWE Raw*.

George Hargreaves: The man behind 'So Macho' founded the Scottish Christian Party in 2006. 'I was a hedonistic sinner,' he told the *Scotsman* about his previous life in the music business. 'I was Jack the lad. I read a bible from cover to cover and I changed my life.'

Mezhgan Hussainy: Simon's fiancée has her own make-up range called 'Me by {me}zghan', and is working on her autobiography. On her website, she describes herself as, 'an icon in the makeup world'.

Leon Jackson: The fourth *X Factor* winner is currently recording new material – he describes it 'acoustic and guitar-led' – and plans to release it independently.

Randy Jackson: The *American Idol* judge is also executive producer of MTV show *America's Best Dance Crew*.

John and Edward ('Jedward'): Got to Number 2 with their debut single 'Under Pressure (Ice Ice Baby)'. Then Sony chose not to renew their one-single deal. Now signed to Universal.

Stanley Kubrick: The film director moved into the Cowells' home Abbots Mead in the mid-sixties. He died in 1999 after completing *Eyes Wide Shut* with Tom Cruise and Nicole Kidman.

JLS: The boy band who were runners-up in *The X Factor* won two BRIT awards in 2010 for best song and breakthrough act.

Adam Lambert: Simon Cowell thought Lambert should have won the eighth series of *American Idol*. Released his second album in 2009, featuring one track written by Justin Hawkins, ex-singer with Brit falsetto rockers The Darkness.

Leona Lewis: The *X Factor* winner went on to record the main theme for James Cameron's sci-fi epic *Avatar*. In 2010 she recorded a duet with *American Idol* runner-up Jennifer Hudson for the second *Sex in the City* movie.

Michelle McManus: The second winner of *Pop Idol* is now a presenter on *The Hour*, a Scottish version of *The One Show* broadcast on STV.

Piers Morgan: The *Britain's Got Talent* judge is also the host of the *Life Stories* series. As well as Simon Cowell, he's interviewed Michael Winner, Joan Collins and Geri Halliwell on the show.

Sharon Osbourne: The former *X Factor* judge is now a novelist. Her first book, called *Revenge*, was published in March 2010.

Peter Powell: The former Radio 1 DJ once introduced Wonder Dog on *Top of the Pops*. Now in 'talent management', he numbers among his clients Simon Cowell, Ant and Dec and Piers Morgan.

Ellis Rich: Simon's first business partner at E&S Music went on to become chairman of the Performing Rights Society.

Jackie St Clair: The former model is still often snapped with Simon at parties and functions, often referred to as a 'mystery woman'. In 2009 Simon gave her a giant-sized picture of his face for her fiftieth birthday.

George Sampson: The young dancer who won *Britain's Got Talent* has since appeared in BBC drama series *Waterloo Road* and the film *Streetdance 3D*.

Ryan Seacrest: The *American Idol* host and radio presenter is also executive producer of TV shows such as

Keeping Up with the Kardashians and *Jamie Oliver's Food Revolution*.

Terri Seymour: Simon's former girlfriend interviewed Simon and Mezhgan Hussainy about their romance in February 2010 for *Extra* in the US.

Sinitta: She got married to businessman Andy Wilner in 2002 and adopted two children in 2008. The couple split up in 2009 after Wilner moved to Hong Kong.

Jordin Sparks: The teenager was the sixth American Idol. She's since been in Disney kids' show *The Suite Life on Deck*, appearing as herself in an episode called 'Crossing Jordin'.

Ruben Studdard: The second winner of *American Idol* has since appeared on stage in *Ain't Misbehavin'* and on film in *Scooby Doo 2: Monsters Unleashed*.

Kate Thornton: The former *X Factor* presenter is now a regular on ITV's *Loose Women*.

Harry Thumann: The German electronics expert was the real brains behind the Wonder Dog singles. He died in 2001.

Carrie Underwood: The *American Idol* winner has won five Grammy Awards since 2005 and is one of the competition's greatest success stories.

Louis Walsh: The Irishman is still a judge on *The X Factor* and manages Westlife, Shayne Ward and Jedward.

Shayne Ward: The Manchester-born *X Factor* winner hasn't released any new material since 2007. A new album is pencilled in for 2010.

Pete Waterman: He was awarded the OBE in 2004. In 2010 he produced the UK entry for the Eurovision Song Contest.

Westlife: The group celebrated their tenth anniversary with a huge concert in Croke Park, Dublin, in front of more than 80,000 fans.

Will Young: The original Pop Idol has had a successful career in music, theatre and film since his win. His song 'Leave Right Now' has since been used on *American Idol* when contestants are booted off the show.

And finally, Simon Cowell: Love him or loathe him, he's changed the world.

BIBLIOGRAPHY

Stanley Kubrick, A Biography – John Baxter
(HarperCollins 1997)
I Don't Mean To Be Rude, But … Simon Cowell (Ebury
Press 2004)
Dreams That Glitter – Girls Aloud (Corgi Books 2008)
Joan Collins: The Biography of an Icon – Graham Lord
(Orion 2007)
Susan Boyle: Living The Dream – John McShane
(John Blake Publishing 2010)
Extreme – Sharon Osbourne (Time Warner Books 2005)
England's Dreaming – Jon Savage (Faber and Faber 1991)
Our Story – Westlife (Harper 2008)
Anything Is Possible – Will Young (Contender Books 2002)